The Puckerdilly Kiss

On the Branches of the Mustard Tree

Teressa Ledford Woodard

ABOUT THE COVER

The cover photo, captured in June of 1955, is my father Rex Ledford embracing my mother Marie Cherry.

ISBN-13:978-1976507236
ISBN-10:1976507235

DEDICATION

This book is dedicated to
Margie Cherry, who was my precious Granny Cherrio,
Rex and Marie Ledford, my parents,
and all the other branches of the mustard tree, my family.

ACKNOWLEDGMENTS

My sincerest thanks to:

My BFF Kathy Reynolds for crying with me, laboring beside me and
correcting my grammar,

My husband Stan for loving me, empathizing with my tears and being
patient with my long work hours,

Robert and Patricia Marsh for reading the first draft and giving their
input.

CONTENTS

Preface (From the Author)

My father, Rex Ledford, had developed the ability to captivate an audience like few people I have ever met. Not only were his stories unbelievable and true, he recounted them with a style that left the listener both laughing and crying. I have spent a lifetime listening to and reliving his stories.

I have pondered the writing of this book for over thirty years, however, family and my career as a high school math teacher always took precedence. As my Dad's health began to decline in his early seventies, the book became more of a priority. At my prodding, he penciled a few stories, but that proved to be a labor-intensive process for him. I captured a few stories on video and finally, I purchased a voice recorder and insisted he use it. It has taken five years to collect the stories you are about to read.

I have spent countless hours and shed many tears reliving my father's life as I attempted to capture the essence of his style and document his adventures in a readable format. I have tried to assume his persona as the writer. My daddy died one month before the book was completed, but he did get to read the skeleton of it.

The stories are not necessarily in chronological order. Do visit thepuckerdillykiss.com for videos, slide shows, numerous pictures of the family, and even listen to my father telling stories himself. This work is a labor of love for my family. I hope you enjoy reading his stories as much as I have enjoyed watching "that crazy Rex Ledford" tell them.

1-Cat and Mouse

"Don't move," I whispered to my two-year old little brother Fain as he lay beside me under the honeysuckle vines. I was a little dirty-faced four-year old, dressed only in a pair of raggedy shorts. "There's a snake about to crawl across my stomach, and he's gonna crawl across yours, too. Just be still and he will go on about his business in a minute. Whatever you do, don't move." My brother, clothed only in a diaper, lay perfectly still, in total trust of my softly spoken words.

At that moment, Fear struck a blow at the very core of my soul like he never had before. Only now do I realize, Fear was my constant companion growing up. Fear led to Wisdom, and Wisdom led to our very survival. Even at four, I was wise beyond my years. I had already faced many encounters with Fear, but none as terrifying as this situation. My mind raced, "Is it poisonous? What if Fain screams or jumps up?" As I felt the scales of the snake's belly on mine, I knew one thing for sure: That snake was less of a threat to me and my little brother than my drunk Daddy's Iver Johnson shotgun.

The Ledford men were decent hard-working people except for the weekend. As I saw it, the highlight of their whole week was getting drunk Saturday morning after the night shift ended at the cotton mill and staying that way until work started again on Monday evening. I hated to see Friday come, but when it did, I was forced to set my sights on Monday. I never knew what would happen while Daddy and his brothers were drunk, but in my short experience, it had never been good. Seems liquor made the Ledford men mean, and I think my Daddy was the meanest of all. He was mean even when sober.

The uncles traveled in a pack. During the Depression, work was scarce. The brothers all left Scrougetown in Clay County, NC, to "get rich" working in the cotton mills in Belmont which was about 30 miles West of Charlotte. Shoot, Granddaddy Mark even eventually followed them. Paul, "Shorty" they called him because he was small in stature, was my Daddy and second oldest of seven brothers and three sisters. Eual, Neal, Dave and JR were the uncles I knew best as a kid because they were Daddy's favorite drinking buddies.

My brothers and I were all born in Cramerton, NC, which was approximately ten miles West of Belmont. We grew up there. Harold was the oldest. Since he was two and a half years older than me, he ruled the roost. Fain was a year and a half younger than me, and as the

1

years passed, I began to feel more like Fain's daddy than his brother. Fain was the sweet one. Arlan was the baby. Since he was fourteen years younger than Fain, we really didn't know him that well, and his youth was a little easier than ours. Daddy had mellowed a bit by the time Arlan came along. Arlan eventually spent his teenage years with me in Hayesville and still lives here today with his beautiful family.

My Mama was Lucy Hooper, a gentle-natured beautiful woman from Clay County. She did the best she could, given the situation and stood in the gap for us, taking the brunt of Daddy's drunken rages until I got big enough to be a target too. I tried to protect her from Daddy's meanness, and he would beat me until the blood ran down the back of my legs.

Alcohol abuse made all our lives harder. Mama didn't have the boldness and downright fight of Eual's wife, Shirley, or Dave's wife, Beatrice. Shirley would hit Eual with a frying pan, and Beatrice eventually shot Dave. He didn't die, but Eual and Dave both learned not to abuse their wives. Those two strong-willed women always got even. Both Neil's and JR's wives finally divorced them and left with the children because they could no longer endure the struggle of life with them. My Mama never did fight back or leave home even though Daddy was a mean and abusive drunk. I tried my best to protect her.

Daddy rode an old girls bicycle to the cotton mill where he earned seven dollars a week. My Uncles would take their seven dollars and buy food first and then liquor. My Daddy always bought liquor first, and if any money was left then he would buy some flour, cornmeal, beans, fatback, and shotgun shells occasionally. He never had more than four or five shells since they were expensive. In the good times we survived on gravy, biscuits, cornbread and pinto beans. Seems there was never enough, though, because we were always hungry. Shoot, we barely had clothes on our backs and shoes were a rare luxury.

We lived in a rented slab shack built under the transmission lines that fed power to the city of Cramerton, but we had no power. There was no running water; in fact, we didn't even have windows. All we had were slab shutters. The wind blew through our house, and boy did it get cold in the winter. We didn't even have an outside toilet. I am pretty sure that my family redefined poor, even in the Depression. We referred to that poor excuse for a home as "The house on the powerlines." At least we had a roof over our heads even though it leaked.

While Mama grew up in church, I am not sure my Daddy had ever graced the doors of one. If he had, he didn't listen to the sermon. In fact, I think he must have been possessed of the Devil because he sure acted like one. I had never been to church but, I could faintly hear the ringing of the bells in the distance.

It might have been Mrs. Wiggins or folks visiting from the church who invited Mama but, an old white church bus started coming close to our house on Sunday mornings. By then, Daddy had already delivered the blow that caused Mama to lose her sanity but, something inspired her to load Fain and me on that old Four-Square bus. Riding that bus became the highlight of my week.

The third Sunday later, Mama was embarrassed of the bruises Daddy had left on her face and decided to skip church. Not wanting to miss the bus ride, I convinced Mama to let me go alone. I am also convinced that I had a divine appointment with destiny that day.

As a four-year old sitting alone in that pew, I heard a truth whose revelation saved my life and the lives of my family for generations to come. I am not talking about the salvation of my soul but literally, our physical beings. That saintly old preacher man explained mustard seed faith with a simplicity that caused his words to soar past reason and lodge deeply in my spirit. I left church believing there was an invisible super-hero called God who loved me, knew everything about me and wanted to help-out. There was one catch, however; Anytime you needed to yell for help, you also needed a mustard seed of faith to go with it. He said not to worry about not having much faith since God had already given me a measure.

I had watched Mama plant mustard green seeds and, she had even helped me plant some in my own little garden. Those seeds weren't

3

bigger than a grain of pepper. Mama kept her seeds in quart jars. The way I figured, I had at least one quart of faith and that was a lot of mustard seeds. I thought about that jar of mustard seeds the entire bus ride home. With it being the last day of Daddy's weekend drinking binge, and the fact that he had already hurt Mama, I knew my turn was coming up. Standing under a big Beech tree after I got off that bus, I decided to call on God for the first time before I walked up that old sled road headed home. I lifted my eyes toward the sky, cocked my head sideways, slipped my hands in my overall pockets, and began to pray, "God, that preacher man said that I could ask You for help and that You would help me. Now, the only mustard seeds of faith I have are the ones you've given me. If it's okay with You, I would like to use a mustard seed of faith and this is what I need: If I deserve a beating today, then so be it. If not, let Daddy go easy on me." Daddy didn't even acknowledge my existence that day. In fact, he was nice.

I quickly decided that God was real, and that He did listen when I prayed. I began to pray a lot and one way or another, God always delivered. I never asked God to give me things, but to give me strength to endure and knowledge to do or find what we needed just to survive. I didn't want to be selfish and just use Him, but to this very day, God has never failed me. I have always heard that God watches over idiots and children. Well, I have been both idiot and child lots of times, vacillating between the two most of my life. The truth is, but for the grace of God, I should have died a thousand times over. I earned the name "Crazy Rex Ledford," for a reason.

Wisdom and Fear were my constant companions growing up. Life was hard. I learned to hear and heed His Voice of Wisdom. God guided me when Fear tried to paralyze me. I learned to keep a cool head in the face of Fear. Wisdom taught, "Drunks aren't very coordinated." Fear taught, "Sometimes they accidently hit their target." It was a simple lesson that I learned well because Daddy was an uncoordinated drunk with a shotgun virtually every weekend. I knew that if something didn't change, eventually somebody was going to get hurt. Something did change.

I learned to play a game with my Daddy that I called "Cat and Mouse." Daddy was the cat with a shotgun, and I was the mouse at which he aimed. I could have died in any given game, but at the time, I was just playing a game trusting my super hero to keep me safe. I played Cat and Mouse with my Daddy a lot that summer, and I got good at it. I knew I would always win with God watching over me. When Daddy managed to make it through Friday and Saturday without being too banged up from fights with his drunk brothers, seems he always ended up trying to shoot something, and by that time, it was usually me.

After two solid days of drinking, my Daddy couldn't hit the broad side of a barn with that shotgun and I counted on it. I counted his shells, too. When the game began, he usually fired the first shot in the house. That's when Mama would grab Fain and then she and Harold would seek the shelter of the woods behind our house. Fain was still a baby in diapers.

The game was always the same. Daddy would eventually stumble outside with the gun to shoot something and I tried to make him waste all his shells. When he came outside, I would make monkey faces and yell at him to draw his attention. As he tried to aim, I would run away and jump behind the dirt pile. His aim was always about five seconds behind, so I was always five seconds ahead of that number six load of lead shot meant for me. ***Kaboom!*** "Yep! Missed again monkey butt!" I yelled at my drunken daddy from the dirt pile. ***Kaboom!*** Of course, he missed again. I ran from place to place around the home place, making him shoot at me until all the shells were gone. That was "Cat and Mouse." To me, it was just a game, and I had mastered it. I always knew exactly how many shells were in the house, and I counted them as he fired; So, I always knew how many shells remained. Daddy taught me my first lessons in addition and subtraction. When he eventually ran out of shells and passed out, we could all go to bed. Occasionally, Daddy lost interest in the game, and we were forced to stay in the thickets all night.

Cat and Mouse worked quite well until one hot summer evening when Fain sat down beside me while I crouched behind the dirt pile. Fain gave me a sideways grin and said, "I play too." Fear grabbed me by the throat! I knew Daddy could stumble over the dirt pile with his shotgun at any second. By myself, I could out-maneuver him because I could run like a deer. In his drunken stupor, Daddy always shot at the first thing that moved, and I was afraid that would be my precious little brother. Pushing past my fear, I scooped Fain in my arms and headed towards the big honeysuckle thicket beyond the dirt pile. I dived under the honeysuckle vines and started boring a hole through that stuff as fast as I could. Fain was crawling right on my heels. After

I tunneled a good way, we just lay there, still as a mouse. I could see the sun shining through the vines. I vividly remember the smell of the dirt, the beads of sweat that trickled off my forehead and, holding Fain's little hand while I pondered the tense situation. I could hear Daddy cursing while he searched for me nearby. About five minutes later, I saw something moving out of the corner of my eye. It was a snake. I hated snakes, but I stayed still. I felt that snake start crawling across my bare tummy. If I had done what I wanted to do, I would have torn that honeysuckle patch apart, stood up and would have likely gotten shot. I thought about Fain. I knew if we got snake bit, we'd probably survive. I whispered to Fain, he was an itty-bitty thing, "Just lay real still," and told him what was about to happen. That snake crawled up on my belly and just stopped for about a minute. I could feel its slick scales on my skin. I think it liked the warmth of my belly. It finally eased off my tummy, across Fain's and then crawled off. That snake slithered across both of our bare tummies while we refused to yield to every human instinct that insisted that we run. God came through again by giving us both the strength to do what was necessary in the given situation. He was still answering the "Mustard seed prayer" as He continued to do throughout my life. I learned at the tender age of four that God is bigger than any circumstance, detail, or obstacle that we must face in life. I never attended a church service again until I was twenty.

2- Ding-Dong, Dead and Gone

Like I said, my daddy was a harsh man and especially mean after a two or three day drunk. Of course, that was every weekend whether at one of my uncle's houses, ours, or the local beer joint. If we were lucky, he partook elsewhere. If he was drinking at our house, we boys practiced avoidance, that is, we ran off in the woods and stayed gone all day to avoid Daddy's drunken rages. We'd sneak in about dark and just hope he wouldn't notice our arrival. The city dump and the Catawba River were both within a quarter mile of the house, and since we were mischievously creative, we always managed to entertain ourselves.

About dusk one summer Sunday evening, we heard Daddy coming up the old sled road headed toward the house. He always came home on Sunday evening to sleep off his hangover by work time Monday afternoon. Daddy was cussing up a storm and just carrying on something fierce. Practicing avoidance, my brothers and I ran to our little bedroom and jumped in bed pretending to be asleep. Peeking out of one eye, I could see that Daddy was kind of scratched up and bleeding. I figured he had gotten the raw end of a tussle with his brothers because somehow, they always ended up fighting when they were drinking. "Where's my '<blankety-blank>' supper you good for nothing woman?" Daddy yelled as he smacked Mama across the face. Mama attempted to busy herself with preparing a meal while Daddy continued his verbal and physical assault. We were all too little to stop him or intervene.

I never understood why he treated my Mama that way, because she was the sweetest woman I had ever known. She did her absolute best to provide us a sense of stability in such an unstable environment. As we helplessly watched, Daddy grabbed a peanut butter mug off that old slab table and smashed it across the top of her head. It was made of heavy, thick, clear glass and had a handle on the side. I am not sure where we got that mug because we never had peanut butter in the house. Who knows? Maybe it was a beer mug. I am not sure. One thing is for sure however, he shattered it on Mama's head and knocked her out cold. I thought he had killed my mom. I can't remember all the details of that day, but my Mama was never the same after that.

I think it was later that week when my Mom went out into the woods, cut down a pine tree, and brought it into the house. She told us it was Christmas, so we decorated the little tree with whatever we could find. She was so happy, and so we kids were too. Our rare presents were never anything more than a cheap "Dick Tracy Pistol" or perhaps an orange or apple. Most of the time, there was nothing under the Christmas tree. We were too small to realize that Christmas didn't come in July. Fain was still in diapers and none of us were even old enough for school yet.

Mama and Daddy disappeared the next day. We came back home from playing in the woods and they were both gone. Neither of them had mentioned a word to us about leaving. They just weren't there anymore. Harold, Fain and I were left alone to fend for ourselves.

Hours turned into days and days turned to months. We spent our waking hours simply trying to survive. I became Fain's caretaker because Harold mostly kept to himself. When Fain pooped his diaper, I threw it away and washed him in the creek. I really didn't know much else to do since I was only four years old at the most. It wasn't long before Fain was practically naked all the time. Luckily, it was summer.

Finding something to eat during that time was really tough. We never had enough to eat even when Mama and Daddy were there to feed us. Eating just about anything we could find, we survived on berries, fish, frogs, honey locust seeds and apples. I remember catching and roasting frogs over the fire. Harold always ate the back legs and left the rest of the frog to me and Fain. There wasn't much meat on those front legs. We also learned to catch fish out of the Catawba River using just a safety pin. Even though the fish got away more often than not, we managed to catch one every now and then. Roasted bream on a stick, that was mighty fine eating. Basically, if it was edible, we learned to eat it.

Occasionally, we would find a little bag of food sitting on the front porch. Someone knew there were three hungry little boys living all alone in that shack. One day someone left a bag of pintos, a head of cabbage and a can of tomatoes on the porch. We thought the tomatoes were firecrackers. None of us could read but we had always wanted some firecrackers. Since we recognized the pintos and the cabbage, we built a fire and put them on to boil like Mama had. The smell of the beans cooking caused the pain of missing my mother to surpass the hunger pain in my belly. We started eating those pintos even though they were still hard and polished them off before they finished cooking. After finally managing to punch a hole in the can of tomatoes, we were somewhat disappointed not to find firecrackers. Anyway, we went to sleep that night with full bellies.

During that time, the Merita bread man began to throw his stale products in a hole on the side of the road close to our house. I had never tasted anything as wonderful as those stale coconut cakes and sliced white bread. It was heaven, literally. God had intervened again. We learned to keep a close watch on that hole. That Merita bread man fed us often.

There were a few times that we were just flat-out starving. After convincing ourselves that Mama and Daddy were dead, we had also settled upon the fact that we were headed for an orphanage. We became afraid of everyone, especially someone in a suit. Mrs. Wiggins lived about a mile from our old house under the power lines. Harold and Fain had gotten into a tussle and Harold ripped Fain's last pair of little pants to the point that he could no longer wear them. Fain was completely naked, and we were literally starving. We decided we had to make a trip to Mrs. Wiggin's house because she had fed us before. When she answered the door, she peered over my shoulder and saw my naked little brother in the woods with Harold. I asked her if she had food scraps or anything that we could eat. She had nothing that day and apologized to me. I thanked her graciously and walked away when she called to me "Wait, I think I have something. I'll be right back." Mrs. Wiggins appeared momentarily and handed me a half-gallon of pickled beans. It didn't take long for us to eat that half-gallon of pickled beans and even drink the juice. Man, were they good. While playing in the yard the next day, we saw Mrs. Wiggins coming up the old sled road. She brought Fain a pair of little britches she had made for him from flour sacks. He loved his new pants. Mrs. Wiggins was always there to help us nasty, raggedy little boys even though she had four children of her own and barely survived. If there was ever a Christian woman, it was Mrs. Wiggins. I don't know if we would have survived without her. She was the only person, besides my mother, that ever called me "a good boy." I loved Mrs. Wiggins almost as much as my Mama.

Daddy had left a blackjack lying on the mantle of the fireplace in the house. It was nothing more than a heavy piece of lead wrapped in black leather. There was a hole in the ceiling of our house. Any time someone showed up at the house, we brothers would slip through that hole in the ceiling, grab that blackjack and prepare for war. Our worst fear was that someone would try to take us away or separate us. All we had left was each other. Our plan had worked well because every visitor eventually left as we quietly hid in the ceiling.

We were in the yard one day when we saw a man in a black suit walking toward the house on that old sled road. Naturally, we scampered inside to our hiding place in the ceiling. Of course, the man in the suit saw us run inside. Harold grabbed the black-jack on the way up. The suited gentleman didn't just leave like all the rest but opened the door and came inside. After looking around a bit, he noticed the hole in the ceiling and came after us. I think he was a social worker or something, but we thought he was going to take us to the orphanage. He made a big mistake when he stuck his head through that hole in the ceiling. Harold laid into him with that blackjack. After a few whacks, he fell on the floor holding his head. I reckon he decided we were too much to handle so after a couple of minutes of recovery and a few curse words, he stood and yelled, "For all I care, you can starve to death!" I am sure that man was just there to help us, but we were just a little too wild for him. Funny, he never came back.

Mama and Daddy had been gone for months leaving us to fend for ourselves. We judged time by listening to the church bells ring from afar. Many Sundays had passed since we had seen Mama and Daddy, so we made up a little song to the rhythm of the church bells. When they rang, we sang "Ding dong, dead and gone." At least five months had passed when all of the sudden, Mama and Daddy came walking up that old sled road. Cold weather had already set in.

I found out later that when Mama set up the Christmas tree in July, Daddy realized that something was badly wrong with her. A piece of glass from the mug he broke over her head had worked its way into her brain. He had simply taken her back to Hayesville to be with her family. I don't know if he stayed in Hayesville all that time or if he came back to work at the cotton mill and just didn't bother to check on us. Anyway, they were gone a very long time. I never understood why none of my Daddy's brothers came to check on us. We could have died. I figured they assumed that we were with Mama and Daddy. After all, who leaves their babies to fend for themselves?

Doc Killian, the only doctor in Hayesville, pulled that piece of glass from her brain using crude tools. Afterward, Mama regained enough sanity to remember she had three little boys in Cramerton who needed her. She made Daddy bring her home. It's ironic, but one of my sons married Doc Killian's great-granddaughter.

Unfortunately, Mama never quite recovered completely. She was very simple after that, just subsisting day-to-day. I imagine that is why she stayed with my Daddy until she died. Literally, it was my Daddy who made her crazy. We never spoke of the mug incident, our being left alone all those months, and Daddy didn't learn much from his evil ways. Life was always harsh at the house on the power line.

3-Adventures with the Mules

Seems Fain and I were always at the bottom of the pecking order. Even the mule would bite, kick and step on us every chance he got. Daddy could make that old mule do anything he wanted because the mule was afraid of him. I have watched Daddy knock it to its knees many times with a firm fist between the eyes. Daddy was a good gardener and I could barely reach the handles of the plow the first time he assigned me that chore. Of course, Fain walked right on my heels  as I struggled with the art of plowing. After the mule had walked all over the corn in the first row, I had to turn him around to go back. That stubborn mule stepped right on Fain's little foot and wouldn't move. Fain started screaming and making a huge commotion, but the mule just held steady pressure keeping Fain pinned. Mules are smart animals, especially that one. The second that old mule saw Daddy step out of the house, he picked up his foot and acted like nothing had ever happened. He plowed like a professional mule after that because he knew Daddy was watching. Seems every creature familiar with my Daddy gave him a wide berth. We all knew he was a mean man.

Daddy eventually obtained a wagon and taught that mule to pull it. That old mule would pull Daddy to the beer joint and wait on him all day while he stayed there getting drunk. Since that old mule knew the way home, Daddy's buddies would load my drunken father in the wagon and that mule would just haul him home. I think we now call that a designated driver.

Uncle Dave used to borrow the mule and wagon to deliver groceries. He made a little extra money that way. Of course, Dave could never pass the beer joint without stopping either. He was usually pretty soused, but didn't pass out like Daddy. One evening after a stent at the beer joint, Dave was sitting in the seat holding the reins while that old mule took him home. It was a strange encounter, but the police pulled Dave over for drunk driving and then took him to jail. He had to pay ten dollars to get out. I reckon it was okay to ride the wagon drunk just as long as you didn't touch the reins.

Eventually, Dave managed to get his own little mule and wagon. At that time, Uncle Dave and his family lived the next ridge over from our house. He had stopped to visit Daddy before heading home and tied his mule to a nail sticking out of the side of the house. It was Saturday, so of course, Dave had been drinking and Daddy was already three quarters drunk. Per their usual drunken routine, they started poking and picking at one another while comparing the size of their muscles. They were both mean and tough, but moonshine made them exceptionally mean and tough. I had watched them cut, stab and beat one another to a pulp more times than I could even count and then act like nothing had happened the next day. As they continued to consume courage from the jar, I could see a mean fight brewing. I knew I had to upset their routine before they beat each other to death.

I had an awful, wonderful idea. It was a terrible practice, but I had once watched Daddy put turpentine on an old stray dog's butt to make him leave our place and never come back. Well, it worked because the last I saw of that dog was a dust trail as he pulled himself across the hill with his front feet while scrubbing his butt on the ground. As we watched their commotion from afar, I turned to Fain and asked, "Reckon turpentine will work on something as big as a mule?" Fain looked me in the eye and said, "I dunno, but it sure did hurt me!" I hate to admit it, but I had tried it out on Fain. It's just kid instinct to mimic their parents, good or bad. I instructed Fain to slip inside and get the turpentine bottle off the mantle.

That poor ole mule was half asleep, just flicking flies with his tail and waiting on Dave. He hardly noticed when I raised his tail and popped that bottle of turpentine in his butt. In fact, I think he liked it because after half a bottle, he just held that tail up and waited for more. I obliged him by emptying the bottle. Just as I started doubting the success of the plan, the mule's tail began to twitch a bit faster. Then he got to peering over his shoulder looking at his butt. After a few minutes he started hopping and kicking. When the mule pulled the nail out of the side of the house, I yelled to Dave telling him that his mule was running away. That mule headed down the old sled road. Dave ran through our saw barn and then across the field to cut the mule off. Standing in the middle of the road, Dave blocked the path of the fast approaching mule. It was still jumping, kicking and by then braying at the top of his lungs. After waving his arms and yelling "whoa" several times to no avail, Dave balled his big fist to knock it to its knees. Dave wasn't familiar with the laws of physics and certainly not with the actions of a turpentined mule. That mule didn't even slow down, but ran completely over him wagon and all.

When Dave came over the next day, he had a pillow case tied around his head to bandage his wounds and was bruised all over. On top of that, they both had hangovers. "Shorty," Dave said as he shook his head in remorse, "I had to put that old mule down! That thing went slap crazy! Just look at my head! He run clean over me last night and I couldn't even get the harness off of him till this mornin'. That poor old thing brayed all night and kicked all the boards off the barn walls. It musta had rabies or something."

I never will forget what daddy told him. He looked at Dave as serious as a heart attack and said "Loco weed. That thing has been eating loco weed." Loco weed was Daddy's term for marijuana. At the expense of that poor mule, I prevented the fight that day, at least between Daddy and Dave. It was a long time before Dave found out what really happened to his mule.

4-Fascination with Explosions

Like pirates seeking buried treasure, we were always on the lookout for firecrackers. We had found a couple of duds here and there on the ground, but none of them had ever exploded despite our best efforts to set them off. Our house under the powerlines had only three rooms. Mama and Daddy had a bed in the living room, we three boys slept in the only bedroom and there was a little kitchen built off to the side. It wasn't much, but it was home. We pirates hit the jackpot one day and that's when the house hit the ground.

I was about six when Fain and I discovered that we could earn money by collecting the deposit on Coke and beer bottles. I guess officially they were soda bottles, but everything was Coke to us. We spent hours scouring the road sides and scavenging in the city dump to find bottles. It was a pretty lucrative business at first, but it didn't take long for us to find every bottle around. Admission to the movie theater was eleven cents, but once the fee was paid, you could stay all day if you wanted, and we usually did. We worked all week finding bottles, so we could watch movies all day on Saturday and we loved every minute of it. Those were happy times for us. Our favorite movies were Westerns and Gene Autry quickly became our hero since he was a real cowboy.

It was at least three miles to the movie theater, and the trek required us to walk the train trestle over the river. I always laid my face on the rails to make sure there wasn't an oncoming train before Fain and I ventured onto the trestle. I could feel the vibrations of the heavy train through the railing. Uncle Dave wasn't quite so cautious until he had to leap into the safety of the river with his bicycle one day. He lost his groceries but did manage to save his bicycle.

The state had begun construction on a road requiring a new bridge beside the train trestle. They had set a little building on the construction site beside the trestle, but it had always been locked and had no windows. Fain and I had passed by it several times wondering what could possibly lie inside. After crossing the trestle one day headed home, we noticed that the building was unlocked. All the workers were off in the hole beside the trestle, and I just couldn't resist the urge to snoop in the little building. Fain served as lookout while I ventured inside to unravel the deep mystery of the contents. When a box labeled dynamite caught my eye, I had a flashback to a Gene Autry movie and a box labeled with those same words. Gene used dynamite, and he was a real cowboy! When I opened that box, my eyes beheld dozens of the biggest firecrackers I had ever seen. I quickly convinced myself that I had hit the jackpot and surely no one would miss a few sticks, so I only took five. In great anticipation, Fain and I ran all the way back to the house. We finally had our hands on some real firecrackers!

After safely reaching home with our prize, we immediately began to seek a way to explode our big firecrackers. Gene Autry had lit a fuse, but we didn't have one, so I went inside and asked Mama for a rag. She found an old dress, ripped off a piece, and handed it to me without questioning my intent. I quickly ran back outside, punched a hole in the end of one stick of the dynamite, stuck that twisted rag inside, and lit it. Fain and I ran around the corner of the house peeking around just enough to watch the explosion. To our great disappointment, the rag burned up and all we saw was a little blue flame fizzling from the end. "Ah, they're duds too!" Fain exclaimed in utter disgust. "Lay me a stick on the chopping block over there and lemme hit it with the pole axe!" Gene Autry had caused a pretty big explosion with his dynamite, and I figured that Fain might get hurt if it did happen to explode. It was a rare occasion, but I did sense a little danger in that scenario.

I pondered a bit and remembered another movie when Gene Autry had shot a wagon load full of dynamite. Plan B, I sent Fain after Daddy's 22-rifle. I knew Daddy was asleep anyway and wouldn't notice. While Fain fetched the rifle, I put all four sticks in a half-gallon Mason jar and set it by a big honey locust tree about twenty-five feet past the kitchen. Fain and I walked back past the other corner of the house. I guess we were about fifty feet away from the jar. I used the corner of the house to steady the rifle while Fain peeped around holding onto my legs. Aiming carefully, I pulled the trigger. They Lord Jesus, I had never seen such an explosion. Ours was even better than Gene Autry's. Tree limbs and boards flew everywhere. I mean, the sky was full. We fell behind the house and covered our heads while the air cleared. I felt very successful, at least for a few seconds. When the air and smoke cleared, my elation quickly turned to dread. I quickly surmised that I just might be in big trouble.

Daddy had been asleep in the back room. Even though I was having a hard time hearing over the ringing in my ears, I could hear him running into the walls trying to get out of the house. Yeah, I had left that half-gallon Mason jar full of dynamite sitting right past the kitchen. We never wore underwear and neither did Daddy. When he finally found the door, he came running out in nothing but a tank-top undershirt. He ran back and forth in front of the house until he tripped and fell over a pile of rocks that used to be the foundation of the house. The house was built up on rocks about two feet high in some places to level it. The house fell completely off the rocks and slid down the chimney. I had blown the entire house completely off the foundation. We used to have a raised hearth where the dogs peered through the floor between the fireplace and the ground looking for a handout. That wasn't a problem anymore. Not only had I blown the house from its foundation but also many of the boards from the walls and most of the wooden shingles from the roof. The kitchen was just completely gone.

Boy, talk about a beating. Daddy gave me a good one and I did deserve it that day for being so stupid. After I came out of hiding that night, I remember lying in bed watching airplanes fly across the sky through the holes in the roof. That just might have been when I decided I wanted to fly. I am not sure, but it took Daddy, us boys, Dave and Eual three solid weeks of hard labor to split enough wood shingles to cover that house, rebuild the kitchen and replace the rest of the boards. We had to stand to build a fire after that day because the hearth was almost chest high. Best I can figure, the good Lord must have been with us since no one died and it never rained while we were trying to fix the house. Unfortunately, my fascination with blowing things up didn't go away.

Digging in the city dump was another favorite past time. One day, we found an old flame bowl. It looked like a big cannon ball with a neck. Construction workers filled them with kerosene and lit them at night to keep people from running off in a hole. It was empty when we found it, but in our digging, we found part of a jug of anti-freeze. It smelled like something that would burn. Back then, anti-freeze was alcohol, but we didn't know that at the time. I poured that anti-freeze down the neck of the flame bowl. As Fain peered over the neck trying to see how much antifreeze was in there, Harold struck a match and held it over the top so we could see inside. That was a bad mistake. A blue flame shot out of that thing about six feet high burning both mine and Fain's eyelashes and hair while blistering our faces. Harold got a big laugh out of that one. We decided to leave that flame bowl in the dump.

17

Upon his return from a stent in the Air Force, Bill Wiggins had stowed a blue bomb in an old shack at Mrs. Wiggins' place. I guess he had kept it as a souvenir. It weighed about ten pounds, and I had been eyeing it for some time before I finally took it. I put it in a sack and carried it home.

The towers that held the transmission powerlines over our house were about a hundred feet high, so I figured that was the best place to drop a bomb. Fain watched from the ground as I climbed the tower. When I finally reached the top, I told him to go hide in the woods. "Bombs away!" I yelled as I let loose the prize. When that thing hit the ground, little pods flew out and began to smoke. It filled the whole valley with yellow smoke. It made a pretty big explosion when it hit the ground, and it woke Daddy.

He came running out of the house yelling, "What have you boys done now?" He worked the third shift, so he had been sleeping. He kept yelling, "The law, the law! You've done it now! Get rid of that thing!" I climbed down, and we started picking up those little pods sending out the yellow smoke. We threw them in the creek, but they kept smoking. Daddy was yellow all over by the time we had thrown them all in the creek.

When the smoke finally cleared out, I had gotten another good beating. I'm just glad that it was a smoke bomb, because if it had been a real bomb, I am certain that I would have killed us all. I was a slow learner, but the school of hard knocks taught me well. After that, I always made sure I was a safe distance away and Daddy was nowhere around.

5-Just Give Me A Gun!

Another day while digging in the dump, we found a great big bullet that had never been fired. I guess someone had brought it back from the war and just tossed it in the garbage. Anyway, we found it, carried it home and just couldn't wait to set it off. After a bit of pondering, Harold figured out a way to shoot it. He forced that big bullet in a knot hole on a tree, handed me a hammer and nail, then instructed, "You can shoot that bullet right through the tree." He pointed to the primer and continued, "Just put the nail right there and then hit the nail with the hammer." I was a little fellow and didn't know any better so, I did exactly as he said. Well, his plan worked like a charm, and she went off with a great big bang! Luckily, I was standing to one side when I hit the nail. I had shrapnel wounds from the brass casing that exploded. The copper end of the bullet was still stuck in the tree. It took a few days for the ringing in my ears to go away.

One of our best dump finds ever was a big Japanese rifle. Because we were at war with the Japanese, people threw away anything that was made in Japan. We played army and cowboy with it but could find no ammunition. Marvin Martin lived about a mile away and had just returned from the war. He brought big bullets home. Seemed logical to us that he had been fighting Japs, had bullets and that they should fit our gun. He couldn't turn away dirty little boys, so he gave us a couple just to make us go away.

The bullet fit in the chamber, but lacked about a quarter inch going all the way in. That wasn't a big problem because I used a hammer to tap it in so that the bolt would close. I must admit, I was a bit leery about shooting the gun after having tapped the bullet in with a hammer. So, I tied a string to the trigger and sat the rifle out of sight around the side of the house. The trigger was so stiff that when I pulled on the trigger string, I just dragged the rifle along the ground. Granddaddy Mark happened to arrive about that time and saw our dilemma. He was drunk, but never mean to us. We could always count on Granddaddy. He only wanted us to be happy.

After surveying the situation, he told us there was no way to shoot the gun with a string. He continued, "I used to be a pretty good shot in my day. Let me shoot it. Just set me up a can over there on the choppin' block." Obediently, I put a tomato can on the chopping block in the front yard. He squatted down, aimed at the tomato can, and pulled the trigger.

When the gun fired, the whole side of the house lit up. When the smoke cleared, he had little specks of blood on the side of his head and face. He looked at the rifle and said, "My gosh boys, what kind of gun is that?" I told him we didn't know and that we had found it in the dump. "Did I hit the can?" he asked. I informed him that he had missed. "Well, give me another shot!" He ordered. I took the old Jap rifle around the back of the house and drove the second shell in the barrel.

This time, he lay down in the chip yard to take a better rest. When he pulled the trigger, chips flew everywhere, and I think he even slid back a few inches. When the smoke lifted the second time, even more little blood specks appeared on his face. He asked again, "What kinda gun do you boys have?" He didn't ask if he had hit the can that time. He just sighed and said, "You boys ought not do your old grandpa that way." He also didn't ask for another shell. I still don't know what kind of bullets we drove in the barrel of that old gun; however, I do know that the Japanese made a stout rifle since it never did explode.

Hack Williams used to rabbit hunt at our house. He was a kind gentleman, and we loved him. I followed Hack around every time he came to hunt, fantasizing the entire time about having a gun of my own. He paid attention, treating us as though we were important to him. When he hunted, I gathered Hack's empty shell casings and played with them on my fingers. It was a great day hunting when I had an empty shell for each finger. That kindly old gentleman gave me my first lessons on hunting.

Hack used a double-barreled shotgun. With two triggers, it was a sight to behold. I wanted one just like his. Something broke in the mechanisms of the gun that caused both barrels to fire as the gun was closed. The next time Hack came to rabbit hunt, he had a different gun, so I asked him about the old double barrel. He commented that it was broken and couldn't be fixed. I began to beg him for that broken gun. Hack reminded me that the gun was dangerous and that I might get hurt or hurt someone else with it. I reckon I tormented him until he finally gave it to me on the promise that I would use it only for playing cowboys and Indians. Well, I lied like a yellow coon-dog. I was sure that I could fix it.

I got busy collecting beer and Coke bottles to buy shells. Pickings were slim because we kept a good eye on the road sides. It took all morning, but I finally managed to earn enough cash to buy four super double X, number six shotgun shells just like Daddy used when he shot at me. I just couldn't wait to try out my new gun! By the time I made it to the old sled road, I had convinced myself that Hack just didn't know how to load the gun and that it would work just fine for me. I had hidden the gun in the leaves at the base of the big Beech tree where I uttered the Mustard Seed Prayer. I looked toward Heaven, quickly loaded two shells, and sure enough when I closed it, both shells fired. The gun flew out of my hands and landed on the ground behind me. Yeah, Hack was right. The gun had a few flaws. I was so disappointed. I draped the gun across my shoulder and walked home.

Harold came outside and spotted my new acquisition. "That's a fine-looking gun you have there. Where'd you get it?" Harold inquired. I explained to him where I had gotten it, and that it was broken. "Ah, I can fix it in five minutes, don't worry," Harold assured. My spirits lifted, and I handed him the gun. Harold got busy taking the gun apart. After about 15 minutes, he declared, "It's fixed! You got anymore shells?" I gave Harold my last two shells.

Bad luck seemed to follow me around. Daddy was asleep inside resting up for the night shift. Harold popped those last two shells into the chambers, turned toward the house and closed the gun. Sure enough, both barrels went off. Harold managed to hold onto the gun and immediately handed it to me. Daddy came running out of the house and saw me holding the gun. The beating commenced. I came out of hiding after Daddy had gone to work only to find that the full load of both shells had hit the metal bedpost about four inches below his head. Harold had almost killed him! Daddy slept with bricks propping his bed for a very long time. I never tried to use shells in that gun again, but I still wanted my own gun.

Shortly afterward, I tore a picture of a JC Higgins 22-rifle from the Sears Catalog. I looked at that picture every day for a year as I worked to save $12.95 for the gun plus the bus ticket to and from Charlotte. That was the biggest town I had ever seen. After I finally found my way to the store and located the right department, the man behind the counter wouldn't sell it to me because I was ten years old. I was heartbroken.

I meant to have that rifle before I went back home, so I stood outside the store asking every shopper to purchase the rifle for me. After many refusals, a good ole' redneck country boy told me he would get it for me. "$12.95 plus tax," the clerk stated. Well, I didn't have money for the tax. I had forgotten about tax. The clerk, knowing I had waited all day, finally just waived the tax or paid it himself. I had my rifle, and I went home a happy little boy.

Of course, I had no shells for the rifle, but I had a brand-new rifle. A box of 50 shells cost eleven cents. I once again got busy finding bottles to buy shells. I quickly became a crack shot and almost always hit my target exactly. Buying shells took a lot of work, so I learned to take my time and be sure of my shot.

One day while hunting, we ran into some boys from town. They always had money and cigarettes in their pocket. By that time, I was pretty sure of myself with the gun, and so was Fain. He trusted me because he had watched me pop squirrels in the head from 50 yards. The spokesman from the group of boys admired my gun and poked, "Just how good are you with that rifle?" I saw a chance to make some money.

"I'll bet you a dime that I can shoot a cigarette out of Fain's mouth at 20 yards!" I stated confidently. They took my bet and I began to sweat. I wasn't worried about the shot so much, but that I didn't have a dime if I missed. Sure enough, I picked that cigarette right out of Fain's mouth as he stood still as a mouse. Fain trusted me with his very life. Looking back now, I realize taking such a chance was just stupid. We took those boys for a lot of money by playing that game until they just wouldn't bet anymore.

6-I Believe I Can Fly

Tommy was Dave's boy. He was a bit older than me, which at the time was about seven. Upon arrival from his house over the ridge one Saturday morning, he whispered in a labored voice, "Boys, I am worn out. I am just sweating all over." Mistakenly, I questioned why he was so weary. Tommy sighed and continued, "Oh Lord, I've been flying all morning, and I am exhausted." Since Tommy had gone to the movies with Fain and me when we had watched a movie about Jesus, he knew that Mary Magdalene had been mentioned in the story line. He also knew that we believed everything we saw at the theater, and that I wanted to fly more than anything. Bearing a tendency to exaggerate the truth, Tommy could really spin a tale. I was aware of his giftedness, nevertheless, I swallowed his story hook, line and sinker!

Tommy continued, "I went down to the Catawba River this morning and found a cave where Mary Magdalene kept her speed boat. After I drove it around a while, I came back and found her airplane. I flew it, and then just went home and built me one. Yeah, I've been flying my airplane around all morning."

Without hesitation or consideration of facts, I asked, "Would you build me an airplane, too?"

Tommy kept spinning his tale, "Sure, but you will need a motor. You know, a fan that you turn real fast as you come off the house. You have to pull your plane up on the house to take off."

I knew that there was a fan off an old tractor motor hanging on the wall in Martin's barn, so I told him, "You and Harold build the body and I'll go get the motor."

The thrill of piloting a plane hastened my steps as I journeyed to Mr. Martin's old barn in pursuit of a propeller. With a quick excursion to the city dump, Tommy and Harold recovered wagon wheels and boards which they nailed together to create my aircraft. It was a fine-looking plane when we finished the construction. Tommy said, "It's ready to go, ready to fly, but we gotta get it up on the house."

I quickly ran up to the barn and retrieved the plow lines Daddy used on the mule. After a bit of wrestling, the three of us managed to pull my plane to the rooftop of the house. "Now when you go off the end of the house, you be sure and turn that motor real fast. Don't fly too far 'till you get used to it," Tommy instructed.

"Oh, I won't. I'm just gonna fly here around the holler till I figure everything out," I stated reassuringly. Tommy and Harold held my plane poised on the roof top as I climbed inside and excitedly prepared for my first flight. I had that fan motor humming when I commanded, "Turn her loose!"

Of course, my plane went just as straight into the ground as it could possibly go. Wow, I was in the twilight zone for a while. With my head spinning and my ears ringing, Harold led me around the yard for about thirty minutes while I gathered my senses pondering what went wrong. I realized that I had been duped. From that day forward, I labeled Tommy Ledford as a liar. I never again believed a word out of his mouth, but that didn't change the fact that I still wanted to fly.

There was a training area for fighter planes and gliders near my house. I spent many hours lying on my back just watching planes fly because it took me away from the problems of growing up in such agony and pain. I longed for the day that I could take a ride in a real airplane. Eventually, I talked Fain into going to the airport.

We had managed to get our hands on some old bicycles when Fain and I peddled a half day's journey to make our first visit to that airport. Upon arrival, we found an old broken-down fighter plane sitting in the field and climbed in as though it belonged to us. After playing with the controls and pretending to fly for a good while, the manager of the airport peered into the plane. We were terrified, but he was a kindly old gentleman. I had developed a good sense for quick judgement of character by then. "Have you boys ever taken a ride in an airplane?" he asked. I confided that we had never even seen a real airplane on the ground until today. "Would you boys like to take a flight?" He continued. I would have sold my soul and Fain's too for a ride. "If you boys will pick up the rocks on the runway, I will take you for a spin." Well, that suited us the best in the world! That was certainly a reasonable trade. With great anticipation, Fain and I worked the rest of that day and most of the next throwing rocks off that red dirt strip. Late that afternoon, the old gent came to get us. "Come on boys, let's take a ride!"

We flew in an old J3 Piper Cub. It had a skid rather than a tail wheel. I will never forget the feeling when we left the ground for the first time. I know now from my own piloting experience that pilots get somewhat of a thrill when taking a passenger for their first flight. The pilot was thrilled, and I was too. My dreams were coming true. After

24

asking where we lived, he flew down the Catawba River toward our old house. Everything seemed so small from the air and for the first time in my life, I felt so free. Oh, how I loved every second of my new-found freedom. Fain didn't fare as well. He got sick. That first experience only made me dream of flying even more.

Fain didn't like airplanes too much after that, but he always went with me where ever I ventured. We frequented the airports around us even making the fifteen-mile journey to Douglas Municipal Airport in Charlotte. The airport wasn't very big back then, so we could get away with climbing in the planes to play with the controls and look at the instruments. I loved the smell of an airplane, especially the aviation fuel. We spent hours entertaining ourselves in the planes.

After a visit to Douglas Municipal one day, we stopped by Airport Park, another little strip close to the house. There was a small carnival going on there, but it cost a quarter to get in. Of course, we didn't have a quarter much less two. After scoping the place out a bit, I found a way to sneak in.

Neither of us had ever seen a llama before, but they had one. It chewed its cud like a cow. After watching the llama for a few minutes, Fain couldn't resist the urge to aggravate it. Boy, he made that thing mad tossing small rocks at its back. Eventually, it started stomping its feet and kicking dirt at Fain, but he just kept messing with the llama. As a very refined woman approached with her baby, Fain ceased his torment of the poor creature.

That lady looked as if she had just stepped out of the beauty parlor. In fact, she was quite beautiful. As she pointed and said to her child, "Oh, look at the pretty little deer," that agitated llama walked over to her and launched his big cud of grass at her. To our dismay, it stuck to the side of her face. Llama spit ran down her cheek before she moved safely away, placed her child on the ground, and removed the sticky, slimy mess with a Kleenex she retrieved from her shoulder bag. She didn't think the situation was very funny, but boy we did. We fled the scene.

Shortly, we became very interested in a little monkey lying on its back sunning. Of course, we had never seen a monkey and of course, Fain couldn't leave it alone either. He whispered, "Watch this." Before I could do anything, he picked up an old dirty burlap sack, snuck over to that little monkey, and then flailed it with that old dusty sack. Man alive, that monkey had reflexes like lightning. Fortunately, it was secured by a relatively short chain or that screaming monkey would have gotten him. I decided that we'd better get on home before Fain got killed or we ended up in jail. That was quite a day of excitement for us. I frequented the airports around the area until I left home years later.

7-School: The Unfriendly Place

I never did care much about school and didn't do it very well. Putting me in a classroom was like locking up a wild animal. In fact, I ran away during recess on my first day. Daddy gave me a good whipping and carried me back to school. I quickly decided that school was the lesser punishment. I wasn't stupid, but I did have a hard time hearing and got bullied a lot. Most of the kids and many of the teachers made fun of me. Seems poor, dirty, backward kids didn't fit in there very well.

Since we swam in the Catawba River a lot, I kept an ear infection. Before I started school, I had gotten a severe ear infection that lasted all summer. Man, that ear hurt. I remember laying my head on the warm rocks since the heat made my ear feel better. We didn't go to the doctor for anything. Eventually, my eardrum burst, and I went completely deaf in my right ear. Much of the time, I couldn't hear what the teacher was saying and that made learning tough. I spent a lot of time just day dreaming while class was in session.

Seems school was a prison for me most of the time since I was barefoot, unkempt, and hungry. I always felt lesser than, because the kids made fun of me a lot. It really hurts when people ridicule and tease day in and day out. I guess it eventually warped me because I had an awful inferiority complex.

Alfred Kitchens was one of the biggest bullies I ever faced. He picked on me every time we met. Unfortunately, that was every day, because we rode the same school bus. The bus driver began waiting on Alfred every day while he chased me down and beat me up when I got off the bus. Man, that was awful and cruel. What kind of grown man would do that to a little child? Alfred Kitchens beat me up daily for a long time and then Daddy would beat me again for being late from school.

I finally got to pondering at school one day and decided that I had to do something about Alfred Kitchens. I was fed up with his bullying. When I got off the bus that evening, I took off running as usual. And, as usual, Alfred was running right behind me. He was much bigger than me, but when he was about to tackle me once again, I stopped dead in my tracks and planted my fist right on that big nose of his with every bit of force I could muster! Oh, the blood flew! Alfred jumped up and tried to run back to the bus. Well, I caught him and gave him a good beating! I kept flailing him until the bus driver finally drove off and left him. Alfred walked home bruised and bleeding that day and he never laid a hand on me again.

I happened upon Alfred bullying Fain down at the Catawba River one day after that. I was overtaken with rage! Even though I was smaller, I walked over, picked Alfred up and threw him in the river! All that anger from before flooded back. Man, I was mad. Well, I didn't know Alfred couldn't swim. He splashed around and went under a few times before I finally had to jump in and save him. I didn't like Alfred at all, but I didn't want to kill him. Alfred always gave me a wide berth any time he saw me after that. I gained a lot of respect that day on the Catawba. Word spread around to the kids at school about what I had done to Alfred at the river. The kids didn't pick on me quite so much afterwards because they thought I was crazy! We all must choose to face our Goliaths rather than shrink and tremble in fear at the size of a giant. And sometimes, we must choose to defeat someone else's giant. Little did I realize; I would face many giants in the years to come.

Fain didn't fare much better than I did when he started school. The kids picked on him too. Since we both hated being there, we started playing hooky at least a few days a week. To fool Mama and Daddy, Fain and I would get up in the morning, acting as if we were going to school. When the school bus arrived, we just hid in the woods. After playing all day, Fain and I would come out of hiding and go home.

Mama and Daddy never knew we weren't at school until we played hooky for thirty days in a row and the principal showed up at the house. Boy, did we get in trouble, especially after the principal got stuck on the old sled road and Daddy had to pull his car out with the mule. After that beating from Daddy, we never skipped school again.

I did have a few good memories of school. My favorite teacher was Mrs. MacDonald. She was a stern woman and gave me several good paddlings, however, she always explained to me why I needed it and what I had done to deserve it. None of the other teachers ever did. They just whipped me.

Every morning in the fourth grade, Mrs. MacDonald started our day with the Pledge of Allegiance and a Bible story. In fact, she is the one who taught me most about the Bible. She took a genuine interest in me, so I tried especially hard to listen and learn from her. She taught me more that year than all the other teachers put together. It was in her class that I almost won the end of year spelling contest. I missed 'gnat' and 'opossum,' so I took second, but I did gain some respect from my classmates as being kind of smart. I liked Mrs. MacDonald. She was a good woman who always gave her best for each student. She treated me like I was somebody and I loved her for that.

Rex in 5th grade

Then there was Old Mrs. Baines. I don't remember much about her class but winning the ugly man contest. I guess I was pretty ugly with my long, shaggy hair, little rusty feet, and raggedy clothes. The class elected me ugly king and poor little Nellie Burch, they made her queen. She was a lot like me. She was kind of nasty and didn't have much either. Thinking back on it now, I can't imagine a teacher doing such to a little kid, but I guess I was just glad to finally win at something.

Denny Williams friended Fain and me. Denny's family had money, so he would sometimes go down to a little café down by the railroad tracks for lunch. Occasionally, he would invite us to go with him. Denny would get a hotdog or sandwich while Fain and I just sat with him. There was always a bottle of ketchup on the table. Fain and I would eat the whole bottle every time we had lunch with Denny because we rarely ever had money to buy anything from the menu. Boy, that ketchup was good. Even still today, I sometimes just eat ketchup by itself. My daughter Teressa, a teacher herself, tells me that children can now eat lunch and breakfast for free at school and that some students attend school, so they can have hot meals. I gladly pay taxes to support such programs. It's never the kids' fault because they have no money to buy food.

Denny had a pair of boots that laced all the way up to the knees. They even had a little knife pocket on the side. That was the finest pair of boots I had ever seen, and I wanted a pair so badly. I knew I could never afford a pair of boots like that, but that still didn't stop me from wanting a pair.

While digging in the dump one summer day, I found a boot just like Denny's. The bottom had a hole in the sole, but the top still looked good. Wow, I felt as though I had hit the jackpot. Excitedly, I kept digging through the trash until I found the other one. It had a hole in the sole too but, I didn't care. After cutting cardboard to fit the insoles of those boots, I wore them around strutting like a prince. I was as proud of those boots as I would be of a new automobile today. The cardboard worked great until it rained. Eventually that summer, the entire front half of the soles wore off and I had nothing left to hold the cardboard in place. Rummaging through Mr. Martin's barn, I had spied a pair of rubber overshoes hanging on the wall. That generous-hearted old farmer gave me his overshoes, so I slipped them over the boots and kept wearing them. The rubber made my feet sweat tremendously, and the truth was the overshoes held the boots and cardboard together.

I showed up at school that fall wearing my cardboard-soled boots held together only by the rubber overshoes. After a few days, the teacher gently reminded me that overshoes should be left at the door and instructed me to take off the overshoes and leave them out front. I told her that I had rather not, but she insisted, and I obeyed. I walked outside, left the overshoes beside the door and returned to my desk. As I walked back in, I noticed her quick glance at my toes sticking through the bottoms of the boots. Momentarily, she nonchalantly strolled back over to my desk and whispered, "I am going to give you special permission to wear your over boots. You can go put them back on." I was thankful that my teacher did her best to preserve my dignity that day and made an exception to a hard, fast rule. I am glad that she realized there is always an exception to a rule, and exceptions should be handled on a case-by-case basis. She had wisdom and regard for my well-being. I was simply doing my absolute best under the given circumstances.

Not long afterward, I got a job delivering milk. Per my best recollection, I think I was only ten years old. Every morning before school, I delivered 250 quarts of milk, and it paid 50 cents per day. That doesn't seem like much now, but it was more money than I had ever had before. Typically, I had spent all my wages by the weekend buying lunch for Fain and me and by slipping Mama a bit of money too. Occasionally I had a bit of money left over by Saturday, when I would visit the dime store to buy Mama presents. I began buying her a collection of the cutest little glasses I had ever seen. I didn't know at the time, but I was buying shot glasses. Fortunately, I just thought they were pretty and she did too. I bought every different shot glass available at the dime store.

Mama always loved my presents. She was simple after Daddy hit her with the peanut butter mug, but she certainly realized that I was trying to show her my love as best I could. Even when she was in the nursing home after she had completely lost her mind, I still took her little presents. I loved my Mama so much, and it seems that life was unfair in dealing her a hand she didn't deserve. The little bit of money I made delivering milk before school sure helped make our lives a bit easier.

Leroy Hester was my best friend at school. Leroy was a fine fellow. He always took up for me and treated me like his equal. He was the one person I could lean on. I rarely shared with anyone the hardships I endured at home, but I had told Leroy about my extreme home life. Despite my circumstances and the fact that he sometimes got teased for being my friend, Leroy Hester always showed me kindness and stuck by me through thick and thin. When my first son was born, I knew the moment that I gazed into his dark brown eyes, that my son would grow to be a man of great kindness. I thought of Leroy Hester at that moment and remembered the great kindness he had shown me. I never saw Leroy Hester again after our school days, but I named my first son after him because knowing Leroy Hester was probably the best thing that ever happened to me during my school years. His kindness eased my day-to-day struggle for survival.

By the time I entered the sixth grade, I had finally adjusted to school, my harsh life and was generally managing well under the given circumstances. Unfortunately, that's the year I had my first male teacher, Mr. Hines. In my opinion, he was a gruff, bitter old man who should have never been allowed in the classroom. Exposing our impressionable children to people like Mr. Hines can only serve as a detriment to their well-being. Life has enough negativity without mandating that our children be subjected to such every day for an entire year. Anyway, I can't remember

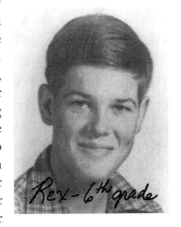

Rex - 6th grade

exactly what Mr. Hines thought I had done to deserve punishment, but he had decided that I needed a whipping for it. By that time in my life I was a stout boy who had learned to stand up for himself, so I calmly and confidently expressed my stance that no other man besides my Daddy had ever whipped me and that he wasn't going to be the first. I didn't really have a problem with authority in general, just with people who wanted to give a beating just because they could. In diplomacy, I offered to compromise by allowing one of the lady teachers from across the hall to paddle me. Of course, that didn't sit well with Mr. Hines and he decided to whip me despite my objections. We had a little run-in to say the least. Mr. Hines couldn't and didn't deliver the whipping that day and thus the principal encouraged me to leave school. Unfortunately, I listened to their suggestions and quit school that day. In those days, a person could quit school whenever they chose. Fortunately, I was already wiser than most grown men because the school of hard knocks had already afforded me a great education. I now understand that at that point in my short life, I held little respect for older men because I had been so greatly abused by the one I should have been able to trust the most, my father.

8-Playing in the Catawba

The Catawba River was an endless source of entertainment for us. In fact, we spent most of our young lives there both hiding and playing. We learned to stay out of Daddy's way and we taught ourselves to swim. A lot happened on the river, both good and bad. Most of the time, what happened on the river, stayed on the river.

I always wanted a real fishing rod like the people I saw fishing off the bridge, but I knew that wasn't a possibility. I decided to just make me one. Mrs. Wiggins sewed a lot and she gave me an empty thread spool. I took a nail and drove that spool onto a straight stick and used wire to make the eyes. I fashioned a little handle on the spool and found some tangled fishing line by the river. I bent safety pins into hooks. It wasn't the best setup in the world, but I did catch fish with it. Most of them got away, but I did manage to land one occasionally.

I can't believe we were turned loose to wander about by ourselves while being so small. Mama was crazy, and Daddy was always sleeping since he worked the night shift. One of my earliest memories was of me and Fain floating that river in a round wash tub. The water would be almost over the sides, but we paddled around in that tub for hours just having fun. We had to be very small for both of us to fit in that thing and it still float. Eventually, we outgrew the tub. We were always on the lookout for some sort of boat.

While digging around in the dump one day, we found two big oak barrels. We rolled them all the way to the river. Fain and I could both float in one barrel while Harold navigated the other. We would stand up in those barrels and use our hands to paddle around. Oh, we had a time with those barrels.

One day, Harold paddled up next to our barrel and pushed the front down. As the water flowed into our barrel, I grabbed the front of his and pushed it down. Well, his started sinking too. As I pushed his down, those barrels sank top-to-top and trapped us inside as they went down. Oh, it was scary! We were hung inside those barrels under the water. I didn't totally panic but kept working at it until I managed to get my fingers between the top of the barrels to pry us apart. It's funny how situations like that roll as slow-motion footage. I know keeping my cool under pressure was a gift from God in an answer to my mustard seed prayer. Anyway, it saved us that day. We lost our barrels, but we managed to stay alive again.

We played in the river all the time, but our favorite time was during flood stage. Most people had a better sense of danger than us and ran from the water during that time. We ran to it. The water moved so fast we didn't even have to swim but just float and ride the rapids. We thought it was fun.

It had been raining for days and the water was raging. We were all three riding the rapids. I was in front. Fain came upon a tree growing out of the bank. The water just swept him under it and he popped out on the other side and kept going. Harold, on the other hand, latched on to it and wouldn't let go. He was drowning. I was already down the river, but I knew if I didn't do something, he would die. I swam to the side of the river and ran back up the bank as fast as I could. I climbed out on that tree and pried his fingers loose. He finally managed to get out of the river and we all made it out okay. God intervened for us again.

One day while Fain and I were playing on the river, we happened upon a liquor still. When we got home, we told Daddy about it. He was so excited about the still that he asked us to show him where it was right then.

Now Daddy would pitch an awful fit if he found even a little hair in his food. We took Daddy to the 55-gallon barrel of mash fermenting by the river. It smelled stout of alcohol like it was about ready to be run through the still. Daddy was happy about that. He lifted the burlap off the top of the barrel to inspect the prize. A big, dead, slick-tail rat floated on top of the brew. I thought surely that nasty rat would keep him from drinking any of that awful stuff. Shoot, he didn't even hesitate. "Aw, that rat won't hurt a thing" Daddy rationalized to us. He removed the dead rat with a stick and then dipped his gallon jar to capture a sample of his newly acquired prize. I was the one who gagged as he took his first sip. "Boy, that's good!" he exclaimed and kept sampling. Fain and I just left him there and started playing by the river. He ended up drinking about a gallon of that nasty brew. Daddy's alcohol addiction was so strong that it overrode good sense.

I never did understand how decent, hard-working people could be so transformed by a drink of liquor. I believe the bootleggers must have added an extra dose of mean in the white liquor Daddy and Uncle Dave drank the day the fight with Turtleman happened.

We were on the backwaters of the Catawba. Daddy and Uncle Dave fished while Fain and I played by the bank. We began watching a man walk down the creek while reaching under the banks with a long rod. When he got close to us, I saw it had a very sharp u-shaped hook on the end. We called him Turtleman because he used that hook to snag mud turtles hiding under the washed-out crevices on the river bank. Fried turtle tasted like chicken but was a tougher delicacy in such hard times. Turtleman had a reputation as a mean drinking man.

Seeing that Daddy and Uncle Dave had whiskey, he stopped his pursuit of turtles and joined them for a drink. The more they all drank, the meaner they all got. Turtleman started to brag that he could whip anyone with his fists and that he had a "bad right".

Uncle Dave spoke up, "Well, I have a pretty good left!" As usual, too many drinks led to a fight. They began to push and shove one another and broke out into an all-out brawl. Uncle Dave was getting the best of his sparring partner when Turtleman grabbed his hooked rod and sunk it deep into my Uncle's left jaw. With a big jerk, Turtleman tore a huge chunk of flesh from my Uncle's face. I could have stuck my fist through the hole below his left cheek. Without hesitation, Dave grabbed the rod from Turtleman's hands, threw it in the thicket and proceeded to give him the worst beating I'd ever seen. My daddy tried to stop my Uncle Dave but only ended up covered in blood himself. Dave landed punch after punch until Turtleman could no longer fight. Then, Dave turned on Daddy and beat him up too! Dave ripped his shirt, stuffed it in the wound in his jaw and then stumbled off into the woods. That was the last I saw of my Uncle Dave for over a year.

I am not sure how or why the police came, but they found both my daddy and Turtleman bloody and beaten. The police took Turtleman to the hospital and my daddy to jail. Turtleman's head had swollen up as big as a bucket.

Daddy told the police that he had not beaten the man, and we backed his story. Turtleman died four days later and the police charged Daddy with first-degree murder. We knew Daddy hadn't killed that man and really, Dave fought in self-defense. Daddy remained behind bars for an entire year. Dave was nowhere to be found during that time.

It was kind of pleasant while Daddy was locked up, but survival was tough. At least we boys still had Mama this time. Sam Craig, who owned the Mercantile Store in town, knew us and the kind of life we were forced to live. He had bought our beer and soda bottles for years and always saved the bologna ends for us. When he didn't have ends, he would just cut off a big piece and give it to me and Fain because he knew we were always hungry. Bless his heart, Mr. Craig furnished us with enough food to make it that year and never charged us a penny for all that food.

I thank God for people who see a need and take it upon themselves to do something about it. We mostly would have starved to death that year if not for his kindness. I went back to see that kindly old Christian gentleman after I was grown to thank him for feeding us that year. The year my father spent in jail was the most peaceful year I had ever spent as a child.

Uncle Dave was arrested a year later in Florida and then extradited back to North Carolina. The trial for Daddy and Dave was in Gastonia when Dave admitted to the judge that he was the one who had beaten Turtleman. The scar on Dave's jaw gave credence to his story that he fought in self-defense. Once again, the police returned to our house asking about that day on the river. I took them to the river, recounted the story, and then searched the honey suckle until I found the hook that Turtleman had planted into my Uncle's jaw. After that, the judge acquitted both my dad and Dave. Everything said and done, we were given a year of respite because daddy wasn't there to beat us in his drunken rages. Yes, my testimony got Daddy out of jail, but he came back the same man. It wasn't long before the drinking and beating resumed as usual. The banks of that old river provided us food, entertainment and, even more, a year's respite from the presence of my abusive, alcoholic Daddy.

9-Learning to Drive

The first car we ever had was a '32 stripped down Ford. It ran okay, but it made the Beverly Hillbillies look like uptown folks. It looked a lot like theirs since it only had a hood, a bench-seat, and a slab-board bed. It didn't even have a gas tank, but that really wasn't much of an issue since Fain oversaw holding the gas line in a jug of fuel. Harold was probably about ten, and I was seven or eight.

Daddy couldn't drive, so Harold and I learned in a field by the house. We weren't allowed to go on the pavement unless Daddy was with us and then only for short distances to hit the backroads. I had a tough time reaching the pedals, but I figured it out. I just tied blocks on my feet so that I could change gears and still see over the hood. Daddy did eventually learn to drive, but it was after Harold had joined the Navy. Until then, we drove him everywhere even though we had no license.

Gas was hard to come by, but we would sell treasures we had found in the city dump and cash in beer bottles to buy gas. Sometimes Daddy would even buy gas for us so we could drive him to buy liquor. We had both turned into good drivers. Harold was Daddy's chauffeur, but when Harold wasn't there Daddy had to rely on me.

We could always tell when Daddy wanted white liquor because he would rub his belly and say his bowels weren't working. "I need some medicine," he explained. Harold was gone so he asked me, "Can you drive me to get some medicine?" I assured him that I could. Daddy was a good gardener, so he got busy gathering vegetables from the garden to sell and then loaded them on the bed of the '32 Ford.

He wouldn't let me drive over 15 miles per hour because he didn't trust my driving, and we had to stop about every two miles anyway to let the truck cool because it didn't have a radiator. We sold all the vegetables on the first two stops. I reckon those folks thought that anyone who drove a vehicle like that really needed the money.

Daddy filled our gas jug like he had promised and then we went to the bootlegger's house where he bought a pint of liquor. As soon as we got off the main highway onto the gravel road headed home, he instructed us to pull over and let the truck cool. He ran around the back of the truck and started sampling his bowel medicine. Every time we stopped to cool the engine after that, he did the same thing. We

37

were almost home when Daddy became intoxicated to the point of bravado.

"Won't this thing run any faster?" He urged. That's exactly what I was waiting to hear. She'd run about 50 mph and aiming to please, I quickly reached top speed. I did a power-slide into the old sled road headed for the homestretch. I should have exercised a bit more caution in the little switch back right past the dump because the ruts were deep there. As I fought the wheel, Daddy went flying! I saw him above me about eight feet in the air, so I slowed down to make sure I caught him when he came down. Fortunately, he landed on the slab-bed. I didn't realize that his right leg had gone through one of the boards and that his foot was dragging on the ground. Adding pain to misery, his leg was against the exhaust pipe. He commenced yelling and carrying on, but I just thought he was having fun. I jumped another gulley or two before I slid that old truck sideways stopping and expecting a compliment on my driving ability. After we freed Daddy, Fain and I had to go back and find his shoe. He hobbled around for about three weeks. I hurt him badly that day, and it was quite some time before he asked me to drive him anywhere again.

It was a Saturday evening and as usual, Daddy and Uncle Dave had been hitting the bottle all day. Mama went out to get wood from the slab pile so she could build a fire in the old wood stove to cook supper. She turned over a slab and there lay a snake. She came running around the front of the house yelling, "Gosh, somebody get something to kill this copperhead!"

Liquor always made Daddy and Dave brave! "Don't worry," Dave assured Mama, "I'll just charm that snake!"

I had never known my Uncle to be a snake charmer, so I kind of doubted him a little bit. He grabbed that copperhead by the head and tail, stretched it out and then laid it on the ground. He pointed at it and sternly commanded, "Now don't you make a move!" Sure enough, that snake just lay there. He danced around the snake waving his arms, and I thought to myself that maybe he was a snake charmer. When it moved a little bit, Dave just reached down and slapped it. "I told you don't you move!" he repeated. The snake refused to obey and coiled to strike.

Too much liquor just makes a person stupid. Dave reached down, picked up that copperhead, and it bit him on the left hand between the thumb and finger. His hand began swelling immediately. "Ahhh, I'll be all right," he said while reaching for the liquor bottle. He took a drink and then poured a little on the snake bite. After about five minutes, the swelling began to creep up his arm. Dave and Daddy commenced drinking again like nothing had happened while I began to worry. I wasn't too smart myself, but I knew that a bite from a Copperhead could kill a person. That was the very reason Fain and I allowed that snake to crawl across our tummies while hiding in the honeysuckle.

After 30 minutes, his arm had swollen to the shoulder and Dave started to complain about the pain. Now my Uncle Dave was never one to complain of pain even when Daddy had cut and punched him during their drinking bouts. I knew Dave was in trouble and so did Mama.

She finally intervened, "Shorty, we've gotta get Dave to a doctor! He's gonna die if we don't!" By that time, we had driven the old strip-down Ford until it had only three rims and a tire. Daddy loaded Dave on the back, I fired it up, and Daddy sent Fain and me with Dave to get him some help. Even drunk, Daddy wasn't about to ride with me again.

I knew we couldn't make it to a hospital since it was up town, and I didn't have a license anyway. Shoot, I didn't even know the name of a doctor. But I did the next best thing. I drove Dave to the Fite and Bumgarten Funeral Home not too far from the house. I figured they'd know what to do and I knew for sure they had a good hearse that could haul him to the hospital. After telling them what had happened and seeing our transportation, the folks at the funeral home decided to help. Sure enough, they loaded Dave in the hearse and hauled him to the hospital. I know people sometimes leave the hospital in a hearse, but they usually do not arrive in one.

A couple of days later, Dave came back to the house in a taxi. His hand and arm were still swollen, but they had saved his life at the hospital. Daddy had to pay the cab fee. I can only imagine what people must have thought when they saw that old stripped-down truck coming down the road with sparks flying off the rims, no muffler or radiator, a little boy driving, and one drunk snake charmer lying on the back. I can still envision Fain sitting beside me trying his best to hold on while keeping that gas line stuck in the jug. Dave didn't have much of a liking for snakes after that and most certainly never tried to charm one again.

While digging in the dump one day, I found a beautiful Elgin watch, but it didn't work. I dipped a feather in kerosene and cleaned the insides of the watch like I had seen my Grandpa do. It started working again. It must have been made of 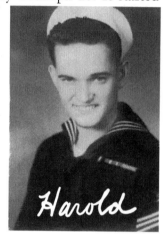 gold because I traded it for a Model A Ford. By that time, I was a great driver and began to test my limits even more. Fain was always with me.   I had discovered that if I hit the hump in the sled road going fast enough, I could get that old Ford four or five feet off the ground. Harold had joined the Navy by then and had left his '41 Chevrolet at the house. Daddy drove it around in the field above the house trying to learn how to drive. He took good care of Harold's car by washing and polishing it often.

Fain and I drove that Model A everywhere. We had been swimming at the river one morning and were on our way back home. As we made our way up the sled road, I glanced at Fain and cautioned him to hold on. I wanted to see just how high I could possibly make that car jump. There was a mud hole in the little curve in the road just past the hump. Little did I know, Daddy had been practicing his driving in the field and had pulled Harold's car under a tree just beyond the curve. I had that Model A pegged at about 50 mph when I hit the hump. Just as we hit the hump, I saw Daddy in the field under the tree just past the curve. We shot at least 30 feet in the air headed straight for Daddy and Harold's car! I knew I had to stop somehow before I hit Daddy. While still in the air, I double-clutched, raced the engine, and jerked it in reverse! Luckily, I landed in the mud hole in the curve wide open in reverse, spun around and only flung mud all over Daddy and Harold's car. Daddy jumped the hood and took off running up the trail by the hog pen that led to the house.

When the engine stalled, I remember the deafening silence as we sat there in the mud hole waiting for Daddy. I knew I was in big trouble! A few minutes later, I saw him peer around the edge of the hog pen. He walked toward us periodically ducking and glancing skyward as if he expected something to fall on him.

We did have several airports near our house and so the noise from airplane engines was common place. With little emotion Daddy calmly remarked, "You boys ought not do your old Daddy that way. You know I have a weak heart. I've been hearing an old airplane skip around here all morning and I thought for sure it had done fell on me." To our surprise, that's all that happened. I think Daddy was just happy to be alive, and he was sober that day.

I later got my hands on a little Bantam Austin. It looked like a little gangster car. The engine wouldn't crank, but by then I thought I was a skilled mechanic and figured I could fix it. Fain and I tore the motor down and decided it needed a set of rings. We both worked and saved our money to order a set from the JC Whitney catalog. As soon as they arrived, we put the new rings in but crossed the plug wires. We pushed it over and over but never got it cranked. We finally pulled it to the road with the mules hoping someone would pull us behind their vehicle till it would crank. We just sat by the road with our thumbs stuck out.

After many refusals and a half day of waiting, two old half-drunk fellows in a '49 or '50 Ford Ton truck stopped. When I asked if he would pull it off for me he agreed, "Tie her on!" I took the plow line off the mule and secured my car to their truck. That fellow took off wide open with me and Fain sitting back there in that little car! The little engine must have been turning 10,000 rpms and it still just backfired like a machine gun. I finally decided it wasn't going to crank and started signaling them to stop. Despite my best efforts, they just kept going! Fain was holding on for dear life, and I was too! I just kicked the car into neutral.

I did my best to hold that little car right behind that truck, but they were slinging us around like a wet dish rag. When they hit the Armstrong Bridge, all four wheels of my car left the ground and we were looking down at the truck bed! I had done that before, but it was on purpose. We came down okay, and they kept going. They didn't even slow down until they slung me wide in a sharp curve, and I lost a wheel. When they saw that, they finally stopped. I thanked them and unhooked the plow line. We were glad to be loosed from those idiots but disappointed that our car didn't crank.

While I was off in the woods trying to recover the tire, someone else stopped. When I got back the fellow inquired, "What will you take for that car?" I figured that it wouldn't do us any good since it wouldn't crank and decided that I should just sell it. Trouble was, he didn't have any money. "I tell you what. I've got a mink coat I will trade you for it," he continued. The short of the story is, I traded that car for a mink coat that I didn't have any use for what-so-ever. I carried it home and gave it to Mama. She said that she didn't have much use for it, so we used it to train the coon dogs.

10-Messing with Harold

I think Harold must have been Daddy's pick of the litter while I was labeled as the scoundrel. I don't remember him getting beatings quite like I did. I think he had convinced Daddy that he had epilepsy. Any time Daddy started to whip him, Harold would fake a seizure and just pass out. His 'athletic fits' as I called them, saved his hide over and over. I tried faking an athletic fit a few times but, he just beat me even more. Come to think of it, Fain didn't get too many whippings either, but of course, he was the baby. I can't remember the number of times Daddy beat me until blood ran down my heels. I often wondered why I had been born only to experience such pain. I had even had the thought that perhaps I wasn't Daddy's child at all. Seemed that I was always Daddy's target when he got mad. I resented Harold a little bit because he was Daddy's favorite.

Fain and I rarely got to go anywhere with Daddy. Despite the polio scare going on, Daddy still took Harold to the beer joint with him. Harold couldn't have been more than seven. My big brother would do a little tap dance or something for the drunks and they would give him money. Seems Harold always had money in his pocket because he spent a lot of time at the beer joint.

One-day Fain and I decided to hide in the back of that old Model A Ford to make the beer joint journey with them. When Daddy and Harold ventured inside, we stayed hidden for a while and then finally mustered enough courage to sneak in through the rear entrance. I will never forget the rank smell of beer, liquor and cigarettes that emanated from that place nor the old juke box that stood in the front of the hallway near the rear entrance.

Daddy called it a piccolo and one quarter played a lot of songs. As we sat crouched behind a table at the rear door listening to Hank Williams songs, we became fascinated by the little bubbles that rose through what I thought was colorful water from the bottom of that jukebox. After much speculation and conversation about the exact operation of that magic piccolo, curiosity finally got the best of us. We needed to take a closer look.

"Sit right here," I whispered to Fain. "I'll see if the coast is clear and then maybe we can go see how that thing works. Run if you see Daddy coming!" I eased my way to the end of the hallway and cautiously peered over the top of the jukebox to survey the situation.

I saw Daddy sitting and talking with a group of fellows at a table on the wall at the far end of the hall as Harold busily entertained them with his dancing.

"Now's our chance," I thought to myself and motioned for Fain to join me. He slipped up beside me and we became enthralled with the inner workings of that magic machine. Mesmerized by the whirring of gears and cogs as that beautiful piece of walnut-veneered gadgetry changed records with silvery arms, we curiously listened and watched those small bubbles rise from the bottom of the glass tubes and flit their way to the top. That piccolo was certainly a sight-to-behold. It was a Wurlitzer 1015. We had never seen anything so beautiful until I peered around the back of it.

I discovered a little slot and saw a quarter sticking out of it. Like a dog snatches an untended bone, I seized the prize. To my amazement, another took its place. I pulled nine quarters out of that magic piccolo. We quickly forgot about the pretty little bubbles and took off to town to spend our loot!

I had hit the jackpot! I thought we were rich! We had never even held that much money in our hands. A quarter went a long way back then because everything was so cheap. We filled our tummies with Moon Pies, RC Colas, a whole loaf of Merita bread, bologna, and bubblegum. After our bout with gluttony, we even bought a gas mask and a pair of Army leggings for each of us. I do believe that God smiled upon us two little dirty kids that day blessing us with a little bit of joy. Doing without does make one appreciate the little things. That jukebox blessing is as vivid in my mind as the day it happened. We came home with the prize that day. As far as anyone knew, we had found it all in the dump.

Shortly afterward, I found an old steel Army helmet while digging in the trash. After giving me a detailed lesson on the structure of Army helmets, Harold convinced me that a bullet couldn't penetrate the steel of that helmet. He put the helmet on my head, backed up a few feet and shot that helmet with Daddy's 22-rifle. It wasn't bulletproof! That bullet went through the steel, ricocheted to one side, bounced about the interior of the helmet cutting loose the headband in three places. But for the grace of God, I would have certainly died that day. I didn't get a scratch. Harold was just as surprised as I was when the bullet penetrated the steel. I have always heard that God watches over drunks, idiots, and children. He was certainly watching over us idiot children that day!

Occasionally, Fain and I did get the best of Harold. One day the next winter, we woke to find that it had snowed about six inches. We had no sled, but a quick trip to the dump produced an old refrigerator lid that would suffice nicely.

We lugged that heavy refrigerator lid up the steep trail to the top of the big hill near the house. Of course, Harold insisted that Fain and I take the first ride. We were a bit reluctant, but Harold quickly reassured us that our make shift sled would follow the trail, avoid the trees, and safely stop in the field at the bottom. Fain and I boarded the lid and he gave us a big push. Sure enough, the sled followed the trail until we were just out of Harold's sight. I don't know how fast we were moving, but we hit several trees, ran off the side of the trail and then off a big bluff. It was a bad wreck, but it didn't put us out of commission. Fain was crying a little bit. Brushing the snow off his little cheeks, I told him, "Don't worry, we'll get back at him. When we get back to the top of the hill, climb on that sled like you wanna ride again."

We pulled that old refrigerator top back up that hill and when Harold asked how the ride went I just flat-out lied. I assured him, "It went down the trail just like you said. Boy, that was fun! Come on Fain; Let's go again."

Fain grinned like Mr. Grinch and climbed on the sled. "Get off there! It's my turn!" Harold insisted.

"No, we wanna ride again!" Fain begged.

"I'll knock you off there! I'm going," Harold insisted again. We acted disappointed and then gave him the biggest push we could possibly muster. Harold took off down the hill, ran off a ten-foot bluff and dead-centered an oak tree. It knocked the breath clean out of him. He rolled around on the ground trying to catch his breath while we laughed in revenge.

The perfect slingshot was a piece of artwork that required much time and a lot of effort. And, making a good one was a day-long endeavor. We had been practicing our marksmanship in Willie Harelson's field but, even with all the practice, I still never hit my target. I picked up an old glass insulator that had fallen from a fence post, kissed it, and then declared with a wink, "This will bring me luck!" I stuck it in my pocket to use later.

Daddy raised and sold game roosters. One of those prize roosters had ventured a bit too far from home. Without hesitation, I pulled that glass insulator from my pocket and placed it in the leather pouch. Closing one eye, I drew back and took aim! That glass insulator took that rooster's head clean off. I couldn't believe it! I had hit my target. My brothers were really impressed too!

Moments later, a sense of dread hit me like a ton of bricks! What had I done? I was about to get beat to death for killing that prize fighting rooster. I quickly hid the body and then begged my brothers not to tell Daddy. I knew Fain wouldn't say a word, but I worried about Harold. He had always been a tattle-tale. I didn't sleep much for a few days in fear that Daddy would discover the dead rooster.

I guess Daddy figured some critter ate the rooster since he didn't mention its disappearance. Unfortunately, Harold began to blackmail me. Every time I refused to obey his command, he threatened, "I'll tell Daddy about the rooster." He took every penny I got for a solid year, turned me into his slave and eventually still told Daddy. Even after all that servitude and loss of goods, I still took a good whipping for the lucky shot. I stayed angry at Harold for quite a while because I felt that he couldn't be trusted after that episode. Consequently, Fain and I kept our secrets between ourselves after that.

Harold had managed to take possession of a little Wizard Motorbike. It was basically a bicycle with a motor. Occasionally, we managed to bribe him with a bit of hard-earned gasoline just so we could take a short spin.

One day, Daddy and Dave had been drinking white liquor and had both passed out in the grass. Harold was gone, but his little Wizard was parked in the yard since it had no gasoline. Seizing an opportunity to ride, I confiscated the liquor jar, poured about a pint in the gas tank and then poured water back in their liquor jar. They were so drunk that I figured Dave nor Daddy would be able to tell the difference anyway. We pushed the motorbike down that old sled road until we were safely out of hearing distance. I put Fain on the back and took off pedaling down the hill. When that engine fired, a six-inch blue flame shot out the tailpipe. With devious pleasure, we roared past Mrs. Wiggin's house and all the way down to the Armstrong bridge.

Our pleasure ride ended about two miles from the house when the engine just shut down. Now, I knew it still had liquor in the tank because it got about 50 miles to the gallon. Unfortunately, no matter how hard we tried to crank that old Wizard, it refused to hit another lick. So, we pushed it back home, stealthily parked it in the same spot, and left it almost just as we found it. Daddy and Dave were still sleeping and never noticed a thing. That was the last time Harold's little Wizard ever ran. I decided that white liquor wasn't much good for anything, especially a Wizard motorbike or a Ledford. In my mind, it brought ruin to everything that consumed it.

By the time Harold had gotten his driver's license, he had traded up to a Harley Davidson motorcycle. It ran well, but since it was missing the brake pads, stopping was a little tricky. Harold just geared it down to stop, so he managed okay. I solved the missing brake pad issue by fastening small blocks of pine to the brackets on the wheel. The blocks worked somewhat, but not as well as real brake pads. At least they would keep the bike from rolling backwards on a hill. That sure was a tough motorcycle.

I could convince Fain to do pretty much anything that I too was willing to try. I do suppose Harold taught me the art of persuasion. I wasn't more than thirteen the day we took Harold's Harley for a test ride. Fain was still about ten.

That big Harley was smoother than anything we had ever ridden. Fain had his little baseball cap turned backwards and was enjoying the ride as much as me. I guess it was the pure pleasure of the ride that compelled us to venture so far from home. I wasn't licensed to drive, but such small detail didn't hinder my pressing onward.

We had ridden that Harley almost to Charlotte cruising down I-85 when I realized that we were almost 30 miles from home and that I should probably turn back. After reversing course heading back down the four-lane, a lady ahead of me in the left lane signaled to move into my lane. I knew that spelled trouble for us since we were traveling faster than she, and I had pine blocks for brakes. Being the quick thinker I was, I gunned that Harley to pass her on the right before she cut into my lane. She had no clue that I was anywhere around. Just as I had almost passed her, she drifted over and clipped my back tire. I must have been running at least 70 mph when she hit us.

In my extensive driving career, I had plenty of experience wrecking but not at 70 mph on a Harley Davidson. This was a new one on me. I managed to correct that first big wobble but only after we had left the road headed up a huge embankment. I had always wanted to fly but not quite like that! I thought about my little brother on the back clutching my pants with one hand and holding his little sack with the other. I knew my driving skills would be tested as never before.

When we sailed off the top of the embankment, I was still running about 50 mph. While swimming amidst eminent danger, life seems to pass in slow motion. I remember peering over my shoulder, seeing Fain sitting in mid-air, baseball cap turned backwards and still clutching his little bag. I was hanging on to the handlebars for dear life since I had to land Harold's Harley safely.

We must have sailed through the air a good three or four seconds as we took flight. As I readied for the landing, I saw old folks scrambling in all directions. It reminded me of the day I almost landed that old jalopy on Daddy. That Harley hit the ground with a force that hurled me from the motorcycle while it kept rolling another 40 yards. It finally hit a ditch and simply fell over. Even though I couldn't breathe, I jumped up and started searching for Fain. Fortunately, he had sailed through the trees and landed in some big bushes which cushioned his fall. Scratched and dazed, he still held that little sack. He looked at me with big eyes and asked, "Where's my hat?" I was relieved that Fain was okay but had no breath to utter my words of thankfulness.

As fate would spin, I had crash landed in the courtyard of a retirement home. As the old folks emerged from hiding and I struggled for a deep breath, I became acutely aware that we had to escape before we ended up in jail. I could hear a siren approaching as Fain and I struggled to pull that old Harley out of the ditch. Like I said earlier, that was one tough motorcycle. After a few kicks, it cranked. As we were about to exit the scene of the crime, a little black boy ran up and grabbed my pants leg. "Hey mister! Hey mister!" He yelled over the engine. "Are you boys some of them there dare devils from the fair? If you is, I am coming to see you again!"

I just grinned at him and politely said, "No, hopefully we won't be doing this ever again." We made our uneventful journey home, Fain never did ride a motorcycle with me again and, that wasn't our last crash landing. Miraculously aside from a few scratches, we, the old folks, nor the Harley were harmed that day.

Harold started working third shift at the cotton mill the summer of his senior year in high school. Soon afterwards, he had traded around and got his hands on a 1939 Ford. It was a pretty car with a little red bird hood ornament. Because gas was scarce, you could get a car for practically nothing. He'd brag to us about that little car and how fast it would go. "Eighty miles per hour in second gear!" Harold stretched the truth. He washed and polished that thing daily. He was proud of it and for good reason.

When gas was available, He and Daddy drove it to work at the cotton mill. When their shift was over, Harold parked it in the yard, took the key out and went to bed. Fain and I had little to do in the summer while Harold and Daddy slept so, I quickly figured out how to jump wire it with a nail under the dash to crank it. Fain and I played in that thing for hours while they slept, but all we could do was back it up and pull it forward since the steering was locked. We backed up one too many times one day and Harold's pretty, little car ended up in the ditch. Helpless, we just left it there.

"Why have you been driving my car and why did you leave it in the ditch?" Harold blamed Daddy as he shook him awake.

"I ain't been driving your car! Besides, you're the only one with a key!" Daddy insisted. Harold just thought the car somehow rolled off in the ditch by itself. He became afraid to park it on a hill. Fain and I left his car in a ditch several times before I stole his key while he was sleeping and made a copy.

Harold and Daddy had walked to work the night we stole Harold's car because it was out of gas. I had been snooping around the proximity for some time and had managed to gather enough gasoline to suffice for a short test drive. We had almost two gallons of gas. Wayne Wiggins, one of Fain's and my best friends, was with us the night we decided to move.

I was sure that with my driving experience, all would be fine. "We will just pour that gas in the tank, take a little ride and, leave Harold's car just where we found it," I schemed. "He will never know the difference." My plan was to just have a little fun and hurt no one. Willie and Fain trusted me, while Mama was sleeping.

I made my way down the old sled road to the pavement, did a bit of low-speed driving to get the feel of Harold's nice little car and then, decided to open her up to see if it really would hit 80 in second gear. Fain rode shotgun and Willie sat in the back. I tried every trick I had learned, but that car would only hit 80 mph in fourth gear. Harold had lied again. And that's the speed we were moving when the pavement turned back to gravel.

49

In my extensive driving experience, cars had never hit 80 mph. That was a bit above my level of expertise, especially on gravel. I went into the first curve moving too fast, and it slid sideways. I managed to correct the slide but then, it slid the other way. I fought back and forth a few times until the car spun completely around, hit the ditch and, turned up on its side. Fain and Wayne immediately climbed out and hit the woods. If they had stayed there, we could've just turned it back over on the wheels, drove it home and Daddy would have gotten the blame. But no, they deserted me.

As I sat by the car pondering, the police showed up in a '49 Plymouth. After a brief discussion, they put me in the backseat of their car. I was petrified. I just knew that I was headed to jail. To my surprise, they didn't arrest me but took me home. When we got to the old road that went to the house, they stopped and let me out. The officer driving said, "Go on home, we'll get up with you tomorrow." I didn't sleep much that night.

Of course, the car was registered in Harold's name and I was an underage driver. They went to the cotton mill to find him. The officer asked Harold "Do you own a '39 Ford?" Harold told them he did. "Well, it's turned up on the side in a ditch down on Sandy Plain," the officer continued. Harold exclaimed that it couldn't possibly be his car and pulled the keys out of his pocket. The officer explained that it was registered to him and furthered, "Does it have a red bird hood ornament?" Puzzled, Harold told them it did. The officer insisted that it was his car. Harold had the car pulled out of the ditch, and he drove it on home. I owned up to the whole story and told him that I would pay him for the damages. Harold continued to drive the car, but he wasn't so proud of it with the side scratched up. That was a bad move on my part and I realized it. I reckon he and I both decided to call an unspoken truce over his blackmailing me over killing the rooster with the slingshot.

11-Breaking Away

Life was always hard as a kid. I was only eleven the first-time Daddy kicked me out. Daddy came in drunk, jumped on my Mama and I fought back for the first time. Of course, I lost. Daddy told me to leave and never come back. I left walking down that old sled road toward the highway not knowing where I would go or what I would do. Even though we lived in an old shack with no power, running water or windows, it was still home. That's where my Mama and brothers were, and I loved them. Leaving was a terribly sad time, but I knew I had to go.

Luke Woods was a farmer who lived a couple of miles from the house. As I passed by, I noticed they were harvesting corn from the field. I just fell in and started helping them. I told Luke what had happened, and he gave me a place to stay. I helped on the farm and earned my keep.

I missed my Mama and brothers, especially Fain, so I'd go by and check on them often when Daddy was gone. It was an empty, empty feeling living away from them. As bad as home was, I eventually came to a truce with Daddy and he let me come back home. Things weren't much different after that. Daddy still drank too much and remained mean as ever, but we managed. I left home for good at 14.

Daddy had been on one of his weekend drunks and tore the house to pieces and shot the place up again. We had all spent the night in the thicket hiding. Daddy had passed out naked in the floor and Mama covered him with a blanket. We laid down to rest a bit just about daylight. I woke up and heard him cursing my Mama.

"I guess you're gonna lay in the bed all morning! Ain't gonna cook no <blankety-blank> breakfast!" he yelled. He was just being mean and hateful to her after we had spent the night in the woods hiding from his demons.

I lay still listening as he continued to verbally bash my Mama. I could take it no more. Mama just barely had time to build a fire in the woodstove when I came from my bedroom, pointed right in his face and declared, "This is gonna stop! This will be the last day you ever come in this house and jump on my Mother! You come in here shootin', tearin' the house up and run us all off. Mark my word, this will be the last time you ever do that!" I had reached my breaking point.

I had decided that I had rather be dead than continue to live in such hell.

I was a good-sized boy by 14. Daddy reached for a metal five-cell flash light and hit me right between the eyes with it. The batteries flew out, and I just reacted. I punched him in the eye, knocking him to the floor! He was extremely mad by then.

Daddy jumped up, ran outside, and grabbed the chopping axe. He came back to the front door trembling with anger and yelled, "Any boy of mine that would do me that way, I'll just kill him!" I knew what was coming when he went out the door, so I had gotten the 22-rifle, loaded it, and cocked it. As he stood there making his threats, I stuck that rifle right between his eyes. He knew that I wasn't joking and was fully prepared to shoot him.

"I don't need no axe to whip you!" he declared as he tossed it away. I pointed the gun to the floor and fired it. I propped the gun and proceeded to give him quite the whipping in the yard. He finally decided not to fight anymore because he knew he could no longer beat me.

"I am leaving here today," I calmly stated. "If I ever hear tale of you jumping on my mama and beating her again, I'll come back here even if I am in California. I'll tie you up and I will bring the blood down your back like you did mine. Don't you ever lay a hand on my mama again." As far as I know, my Daddy never beat on Mama again, even though he continued to drink. Arlan, my baby brother, was born shortly afterward.

Tommy Ledford and I left Cramerton for the mountains of Western North Carolina in Clay County. JR, Daddy's brother, had moved back to Bell Creek in Hiawassee, Georgia by then with his wife and family. JR took us in. Bell Creek was just across the North Carolina/Georgia line from Scrougetown in Hayesville. I loved the mountains. Somehow, I knew that I would eventually make my home there.

I worked various jobs over the next few months, but never really could get ahead. I knew I had to do something better so, I ventured back East and joined the Paratroopers at 15, even though I lied and told them I was 16. I had convinced someone in Hiawassee to forge a birth certificate.

I had never seen so much food the first time I visited the mess hall at Fort Jackson, South Carolina. They had chicken, milk, butter, dessert, and all kinds of things I wasn't used to having. I don't think I had ever eaten all I wanted. *Take all you want, but eat all you take* was what the sign said. Man, I loaded up the first time through and finished that tray quickly. I asked the guard standing by the door if that sign really meant what it said. He said, "Yes, take all you want, but be sure that you eat it." I kept eating and eating until that guard came over and stood beside me. I reckon he was enforcing the rules. "You like that do you?" He questioned.

"Yeah buddy! That's some fine eating," I replied. The guard let me finish and then took me to the kitchen and put me on KP for 24 hours straight. I worked cleaning the floors and washing trays and then had to do it all over again even though everything was clean. I never did understand that philosophy.

They didn't even let me sleep but sent me over to pick up my gear. I was issued two pairs of boots, socks, underwear, nice wool uniforms, and all sorts of new stuff. I felt like a big wig with all that new stuff. I

Rex Ledford in Basic Training in the 50's
Company F, 28th Infantry Division
Ft. Jackson, SC

thought I had hit the jackpot even though I was very tired. Sixteen weeks of basic training ensued, and man, it was hot! I was young and did just fine with the training. It was the crazy rules that got me. I suppose I was the worst Gomer Pyle they had ever met.

After that, I went on a BIVWAK even though I didn't know what that was. I saw it as a nice camping trip where we did training exercises night and day. I always kept a hook and fishing line in my cap.

One day while we were marching, we passed a very nice-looking fish pond. We set up camp about a mile up the road. It had been a long time since I had fished. They instructed us not to leave the company area, but I couldn't seem to get that pond out of my mind. I was hungry, and I figured they wouldn't miss me since there were a lot of other fellows there. I left when no one was watching.

I scrounged around to find grasshoppers and worms to use for bait and quickly caught a big stringer of fish. I made my way back to camp, and my sergeant was waiting for me. Oh, he bragged on my fish and showed them to everyone. I was feeling mighty proud. Shoot, I thought he was going to help me eat them. All the sudden, my big black platoon sergeant looked at me very sternly and commanded, "Get your shovel!" He took me off behind the camp, marked off a six by six-foot area and told me to dig a hole two feet deep. "Come back and get me when you are finished," He ordered. He kept my fish.

I got busy digging a very nice hole. I had moved a lot of dirt with that tiny shovel when I went back to get him. He took me back to the hole, tossed my fish in and commanded me to bury them. "We don't want those fish stinking. Come and get me when you are finished." I dutifully buried the fish and retrieved him once again. "Nice job, Ledford," he commented and then continued, "On second thought, dig them back up." That didn't set too well with me, but I obeyed. The longer I dug, the angrier I became. I had decided that if he told me to dig that hole again, I would bury him in it. It was early morning when I retrieved that drill sergeant once again. I reckon he sensed my anger and told me to leave the hole open and get some sleep. I didn't fare well with rules that I thought were stupid. I suppose that he was simply teaching me to obey orders.

Jimmy Howard was my tent mate on BIVWAK and I was a jokester. Each of us had a half of a tent that snapped together to make one. The drill sergeant had instructed us to look thoroughly for snakes before we set up our tents. Two of our black friends turned every leaf before they set theirs up. When their backs were turned, I broke a thin stick and laid it down where they would place their tent. That night as one of them read and the other tried to sleep, I told Jimmy, "Watch this."

Rex and Jimmy

54

I guess I was just mean, but I wiggled the end of that stick, and the fellow reading said to the other, "Did you feel that?"

The other replied, "Ah man, leave me alone, I am trying to sleep." I wiggled the stick again that was strategically placed under their tent.

"I heard it that time!" he whispered.

I thrashed the end of that stick and both those boys jumped up and yelled, "It's a snake!" They took off running with their tent while Jimmy and I rolled in the leaves laughing. That little stunt was just mean.

Jimmy was a city boy and was enthralled by a skunk that wandered into camp one night. Even though I cautioned him to leave it alone, Jimmy decided to catch it anyway. He ran up to the skunk and trapped it with his helmet. That skunk sprayed him all over. Jimmy stunk up the whole camp and the sergeant made him bury his clothes, boots, and helmet. He learned the hard way not to mess with a skunk. He stunk up the camp for three days and even I refused to sleep with him.

We had to take a class on supply economy where the sergeant put on a little demonstration about toilet paper conservation and declared, "Don't waste anything." I had never really wasted much of anything, but I decided that the Army must be stretched for supplies if they needed to save on toilet paper. I was walking around in the woods at Fort Jackson and found a 105 Howitzer bullet that had never been fired. It was a big bullet about three feet long and I figured it must have cost the Army $75 or a $100. I decided that I should turn it back in to them so the Army could save some money. I looked it over good and could find nothing wrong with it except that it was missing the tip. I thought surely sergeant would be proud of me.

I knocked on the sergeant's door at the barracks and walked in with that big bullet. He instructed me, "Just take it easy," and got on the phone. In a few minutes, the bomb squad showed up in padded gear.

It finally dawned on me that they feared the shell, so I told them, "Don't worry, I'll just take it back and put it where I found it."

I decided that the bullet shouldn't be wasted. I figured that I could disarm it and make a lamp out of it or something. I emptied the shell of the powder and struck a match to it. It wasn't normal gun powder like I was used to. I lit the entire country side up and burned my hair off. I hid the evidence of my folly as best as possible. When the sergeant saw me the next morning he asked, "Did you get rid of your bomb?" Obviously, he knew what had happened. I can only surmise that perhaps he had done the same thing before per his reaction.

I had been in jump school leaping from towers for three weeks when it was time to make the first real jump. I had to walk down a line and choose a parachute from the table. I swapped about three times before I finally settled on one. We boarded a C-47 loaded with 52 Paratroopers.

The whole time we climbed in that airplane, I kept thinking about the time Harold built a parachute for a black cat. Harold climbed a tree and dropped the cat. Terrified, the cat caught a limb and wouldn't let go. Harold decided to set fire to the parachute so the cat would let go. He burned the cat to death. That was an awful thing for me to watch as a kid. I kept thinking that cat was about to take his revenge on me that day.

When the time to jump came, a red light came on. The jump master yelled, "Get ready, get ready!" All I could think about was that cat. When the green light came on he yelled, "Stand up!" Well, everyone stood up but me. I knew I would be a little weak, but no matter how hard I struggled, I just couldn't get up. The jump master came over and unbuckled my seat belt. I reckon he had strapped me in while I was lost in the horror story of the black cat. He said, "Stand up and shuffle to the door." I was second in line. There was a great big fellow ahead of me. He peered out that door looking at those matchbox jeeps on the ground and started carrying on something fierce. Despite their best efforts to throw him out, they finally just gave up, pulled him back in and sat him down. I was next, and thus first.

I peered out the door and saw the little matchbox jeeps. I heard the old jump master say something, and I looked at him and asked him what he said. "I said Go!" He yelled. I jumped out the door and started turning end over end thinking about that black cat the entire time. I just knew it was cat's revenge! I caught alternating glimpses of the ground and the airplane for quite some time until finally "kaboom!" I was sure I had hit the ground. I had always wondered what it felt like to die. It wasn't too bad. I had always figured that it would hurt more. I couldn't see anything but, I smelled sweat very strongly. The fear was subsiding a bit when I realized that my helmet had fallen over my face and that I wasn't dead. I repositioned my helmet, looked up and saw that open parachute. Whew, what a relief. I am not dead. But, I realized that I had to land.

I hit the ground hard shortly thereafter. It wasn't pretty. I forgot all my training from the towers. After slamming my head in the ground several times, a few flips and being dragged by the wind, I finally stopped. One of the sergeants on the ground came over to me and asked, "What kind of a landing was that soldier?"

I was a bit dazed and simply replied, "It was a right-rear, sir." They made us all jump again that day. After several jumps, I figured it all out, but that first one was the black cat's revenge! It was Harold's fault!

I made $41 a month and got a $9 raise when I completed jump school. I grew increasingly agitated with each silly punishment my officers inflicted upon me and grew even more unruly in the eyes of my superiors. I stayed in trouble all the time. The Army finally discharged me from service because I couldn't seem to comply with their rules.

12-The Puckerdilly Kiss

I went back to Belmont realizing I needed to learn a trade if I was to earn a decent wage. I wasn't about to work at the cotton mill like the rest of my alcoholic family. I vowed to myself that I would be different. Since I could tinker with engines, I decided to pursue the profession of automobile mechanic. Seeking to make a deal with the owner of Cannon Ford, I offered to work a free apprenticeship with his best mechanic. He agreed and even provided lodging in the Ford place. I slept on the couch in the breakroom and gave him free labor, but I learned to be a mechanic.

I had exhausted my savings after three months and explained to the owner that I had to get a job. He hired me at $35 per week. After that, I quit beating myself up over my failed military career. I was already earning more than my Daddy and certainly more than a paratrooper who was subjected to constant harassment. It was also during that time that I found my niche in dirt-track racing. I was a natural. After all, I had been practicing the art since I was seven.

After a year or so, I grew weary of the Belmont scenery and my daily hum-drum life. I had dated a few beautiful girls, wrecked a few cars, won a few races, and experienced life as I thought it should be. Yet life was dull and empty. I needed a change. I had no clue as what type of fulfillment I sought, but I headed back to the mountains of Clay County with my race car in tow. I was only twenty by then. Little did I know, I was about to be smitten by a sickness that would send me reeling.

Upon my arrival in Hayesville, I moved in with my Aunt Lizzie, Mom's sister, and Uncle Roy Ledford, Lizzie's husband. Because he was my Grandpa Mark's half-brother, I was related to them on both sides of the family. The family tree was complicated to say the least. Appalachian culture was such that when family needed help, help was given. Since I was family on both sides, Lizzie and Roy took me in, no questions asked.

Aunt Lizzie and my Uncle Roy had reared a lovely family of five: Charles, Edward, Blonde-who had hair as black as coal, Thelma, and lastly Ora Mae. Aunt Lizzie reminded me so much of my mother that they could have passed for twins. I often wondered if I might have had a normal loving family like theirs had my Daddy not broken that peanut butter mug over my mom's head. It was nice to experience how a normal, non-alcoholic family lived their daily lives. I had never known that, but I liked it. I took a mechanic job at Duvall Ford in Hayesville making $20 per week. My wage was a bit of a setback, but I found myself happy.

Lizzie's family attended Hayesville Church of God every time the doors were open. Furthermore, they attended every revival, singing, homecoming or special service which any of the other Churches of God held. There were several churches in the area, so that was a lot of church going. Lizzie always invited me to go with them but never chided me when I didn't. I don't think they ever knew, but I would often venture by, sit in my car with the windows down, and listen to the beautiful sounds that emanated from those humble buildings. That was the closest I had gotten to a church since I had been scarred as a child and prayed my first mustard seed prayer.

It was a sweltering night in June of 1955, when I was smitten. It was revival time at the Tusquittee Church of God, and as per usual, all faithful church goers showed up to support the cause. I sat outside listening from the safety of my car. I was captivated by the alluring voices that emanated through the open windows filling the entire valley with jubilant praise. I was compelled to have a closer look. I left the safety of my vehicle, ventured to a side window, and began not only to listen but also to watch the proceedings that took place inside.

Peering through that tiny open church window, I saw the most beautiful woman I had ever laid eyes upon. Her long curly black hair, dark brown eyes, and the most angelic smile I had ever seen held me mesmerized. Her little pink dress with raised flowers in the fabric was so enchanting that averting my eyes was impossible. Transfixed, I stared as she made her way down from the choir loft to take her seat among the congregation. To my

Marie Cherry.
"The angel in the choir"

surprise, she eased into the pew right by my window. Before she took her seat, she glanced my way, smiled shyly, and then winked at me. Like Thumper meets Bunny in the movie *Bambi*, I was smitten to say the least. Even though I was shy, I could hardly wait until the service ended so I could talk with her.

The longer the service lasted, the more nervous I became. I had spent my life conquering fear and I sure wasn't about to let fear stop me then. When she exited the church, I quickly made my approach, mustered all the courage I could, and then asked using my best John Wayne voice, "Can I take you home?"

She quickly responded, "Wait a minute, I'll ask Mama."

Margie was a God-fearing, wonderful woman who was also a faithful member of the Hayesville Church of God, Lizzie's home church. She cocked her head sideways and peered through the darkness at me. I reckon she thought I was Edward Ledford, Lizzie's boy, since we looked alike. Edward was a faithful member in good standing at the Hayesville Church of God too, so Margie gave Marie her okay.

Marie was Margie's first born. Margie married Pearl Cherry after his first wife died of blood poisoning. She raised her step-daughter, Betty, as her own. All five of Marie's siblings: Betty, Roberta, Pat, Bud, and Susan all piled on the back of a dump truck with their Mama headed home from church. (See Appendix for more photos of the family.) I suppose that old dump truck served as the church bus. I dutifully followed that slow-moving truck until I could no longer bear to do so. A mile from the church, my speed demon manifested, and I sped around them. I couldn't help it; I had always driven like I was in a race.

When I hit the old Tusquittee Bridge, I was going so fast that I jumped the length of the bridge and landed eight feet past the other side. I had been practicing that move since I was seven. I grinned at

Marie looking for some acknowledgment of my expert driving skills. Marie didn't say much all the way to her house. I didn't either. I figured my crazy driving antics had blown my chances. When we reached her house, I walked her to the door. She ruined me for the rest of my life when she leaned forward and planted a little puckerdilly kiss right on my lips.

I continued to visit Marie at every opportunity that summer. I floated on clouds of joy while in her presence and battled love sickness when we were apart. I was head over heels in love with a fourteen-year-old angel. I thought about her with every waking moment and dreamt about her almost every night. I resorted to drastic measures when I pulled out the mustard seed faith. I climbed to the top of the mountain behind Marie's house. As tears streamed down my face I prayed, "Lord, I love her so much, I want to marry her. Please give her to me. If that's not possible, please remove her from my life!" I had neither prayed nor cried in years. In retrospect, I think God was nudging me to yell for help so He could intervene in my life once again. Margie's family was the kind I had always wanted, stable and normal. I wanted that lifestyle. Since I saw stable and normal in Marie, I thought that she could bring that to me.

I decided to pop the question shortly after praying on the mountain that day. Only a couple of months had passed since I had first laid eyes on her. Marie was still in school. She was a smart, popular, and beautiful young woman with strong family values. I decided that if she said yes, then I knew I had my answer. If she said no, well, I still had my answer.

I got a ring and went to see her. "I'm gonna give you something. If you don't want it, don't take it. I'll be back at Christmas and we will get married if you do." To my amazement, she took it. I knew that we couldn't live on $20 a week, so I went back to Charlotte, got a job at

Ford Motor Company and rented an apartment in preparation for my new bride. She wrote in a letter that her daddy wasn't keen on the idea because she hadn't finished high school. I decided not to worry much about it because she had said yes. I did, however, need her parent's approval.

Pearl Cherry, Marie's Daddy, was a very kind hearted, quiet man who deeply loved his first-born daughter with Margie. Pearl was a farmer who worked at Mingus Supply to help make ends meet. Although Pearl rarely went to church, he too held a deep faith in God, but Margie was clearly the cornerstone of the family.

I returned at Christmas, like I had promised Marie, with a marriage license in hand. At least one parent had to sign the marriage license because she was underage. Margie signed it without hesitation, but in my heart, I knew I couldn't marry her without Pearl's approval.

Her daddy was out back feeding the chickens when I showed him the marriage license and asked if he would sign it. Without looking at me he replied, "I don't have to, her mamma has already signed it."

I humbly stated my position, "No, you have to sign it too or I won't marry her. I want your approval." I repeated, "If you don't sign, I won't marry your daughter."

He pulled a small pencil from his overall pocket and signed the marriage license as he relinquished, "Be good to her. She'll make you a good wife." We married on Christmas Day, 1955 at Truett McConnell Church in Hiawassee Georgia.

After over sixty years of marriage, I have realized that Marie has been the cornerstone of our family. She was the one who sacrificed and held our family together. Marie was more mature at 14 than I was at 20 and has been my greatest blessing in this life. Not only did she manage to cope with my dysfunctional tendencies and rear six  wonderful children at the same time, her life was never easy. For years, she labored from the early hours of the morning until the wee hours of night to provide a stable home for us all. Upon reflection, I sometimes feel as though I stole her life. I am thankful that she had the courage to stay the course when changing direction would have been the path of least resistance. I have come to realize that my children inherited their brilliance and drive for perfection from her. It seems to me the only thing they inherited from me was my high-rear end and swayed back.

13-Trying to Settle Down

Times were tough during our first few years. I barely earned enough to make ends meet and sometimes the ends were squirrels I had killed. I bought a little travel trailer shortly after moving to Charlotte, and we left the apartment to live in it. The following summer, I pulled the travel trailer back to Hayesville and set it up in Pearl's backyard. Since Marie was expecting our first child the following March, I wanted to get her closer to home and I knew she would be safe with Margie. I went to Atlanta, got a job at Beaudry Ford, and then purchased and lived in a 30-foot Zimmer travel trailer during the week. Maria Joanne was born on March 24, 1957. Three

Marie and baby
Maria April '57

weeks later, Marie moved to Atlanta with me where we setup home in the 30-foot Zimmer. I sold a calf I had grown out at Pearl's to pay the $75 hospital bill for Maria's birth.

Over the next four years, we moved back and forth from Hayesville to Atlanta living in that 30-foot Zimmer. During that time, we built a house on land that Pearl had given us. I also built a garage and opened my own auto repair business. Growing the business was tough, hence our moving back and forth to Atlanta.

Judy was born December 20, 1958; Leroy-September 9, 1960; and, Teressa-April 22, 1962. Maria, the oldest, was about to begin school when we were finally able to settle in Hayesville for good.

While I was moving Marie all over the place, Fain was serving a three-year stent in the Paratroopers. When his obligation was done, he came to live with us in the Zimmer. He was like my son too, so I felt the need to take care of him. Fain was wild as a spring-buck, and I still wasn't much better. To be honest, I don't know how Marie managed to put up with me, Fain and all the other adventurous friends of mine.

Fain
my Precious
Brother

I had few good role models in my life; so, I really knew very little about being a good husband, father, or citizen. I should have never put Marie or her family through my shenanigans. I suppose God gave Marie the grace to stick by me, since I was a lot like my Daddy and expected her to act like my mother. I didn't get drunk and shoot at the kids, but I had a lot of his ways, and so did Fain. She took care of me, Fain, my friends, and all the kids.

Fain took a job as a handyman at a fix-it-all business in Atlanta. He slept on the convertible bed in the living room of the Zimmer beside Judy's cradle. Fain was like me in that he was a bit over confident in all things. When his boss asked him if he could do plumbing work he replied, "Why sure. I am an expert plumber." Fain had never plumbed anything,

and our own home had never even had indoor plumbing.

His boss said, "This lady wants a sink in her kitchen. She had a well drilled and said everything you need is sitting in the kitchen where she wants the sink installed. Go put it in."

Fain arrived at the home with his little red toolbox. Being the logical thinker, he was, he concluded that the first order of business was to get water to the kitchen from the well outside. After carefully examining the new pump, Fain removed the plug from the side of the well and immediately got soaked. After managing to turn the pump off, he connected pipes, ran them along the ground to the house, and then through a hole he knocked in the foundation. Fain had never seen nor used a pipe-cutter. He simply ran the copper piping through the floor, coiled the excess, and mounted the sink. Despite his best efforts to coil the excess pipe, the sink rested chest high on the wall. Being quite the gentleman, Fain built the lady a set of steps so she could reach the sink. He sat a bucket under the drain so she could empty the bucket off the back porch like Mama had.

Fain arrived at work the next day to face an irate boss. "What did you say to that woman that made her so mad?" The boss questioned.

"I didn't even see her," Fain explained.

"She said she was gonna sue me!" His boss continued. Fain took his little red toolbox and quickly left. Fortunately, one of his sons became an expert plumber.

In the early years of our marriage, Fain, our friends, and I often found ourselves locked behind iron bars. I rarely consumed alcohol but, Fain and his friends drank my share. I was just a speed demon who always ran from the blue lights of the law. Between all of us, we didn't even have a set of valid driver's license. The law couldn't distinguish between me and Fain since we had both lied so much and shared driver's licenses. We were nothing but stupid and wild. Bless Marie's heart, she didn't have a driver's license either. She was imprisoned behind the walls of that 30-foot Zimmer tending to the children and wondering where we were most of the time. I wasn't a good father nor husband.

It was a Friday evening on Easter weekend in Atlanta. Fain had convinced me that he should drive, even though he had been drinking. Long story short, Fain ran my car up a phone pole. He was arrested for drunk driving and I for aiding and abetting. We had been in jail from Friday evening until Sunday evening and had given no word to Marie. I had used all my phone calls to contact my friend, Oscar Parker. After two days, Oscar managed to raise the funds to bail me out of jail but, Fain remained behind bars. I assured the jailer that I would be back to retrieve Fain.

Two days passed before I raised bail money for Fain. By then, he had already been sent to the big boy's prison in Jonesboro. When I arrived there, Fain was wearing a striped suit and was hours from being assigned to the chain gang like we had seen in the movies. That was a low point in life even for us. Seems we were repeating the Ledford behavior I had vowed to escape. My refusal to obey the law and my loyalty to Fain had brought a lot of undue hardship on Marie and my children. On top of that, I was still too stupid to recognize and avoid dangerous situations.

Charles Burdett was one of my friends from Hiawassee. He too had ventured to Atlanta in search of gainful employment. At my invitation, he lodged with me, Marie, Maria, Judy, and Fain in the 30-foot Zimmer.

Charles and I decided to go fishing one Saturday afternoon, so we loaded my little fishing boat in the back of my '50 Ford pickup and headed to Lake Lanier. After several hours of unproductive fishing, we came back to shore and once again loaded the boat in the back of the truck. The day took a turn for the worst when we decided to rent a speed boat from a dock nearby rather than heading home. Six dollars seemed a lot to rent a boat for an hour but, we pooled our money and launched.

Even in the early sixties, Lake Lanier was populated with yachts and houseboats. They made a big wake in the water. I was driving at the time, fell in behind a yacht, and began zig-zagging back and forth jumping the wake. We must have circled and jumped for a good 15 minutes in that speed boat. I had no idea that there existed such a thing as lake police. I reckon the fellow driving the yacht must have radioed them because, that big police boat fell in behind us. It had no sirens or lights, so I thought the driver wanted to play chicken. I obliged.

I had made three or four sweeping passes at him when I realized that our one-hour rental was almost up and that we should head back to the boat launch. I did notice on the third pass that the driver wore a uniform. I just figured he was dressing the part of a ship captain. He must have recognized the speed boat rental from the place we had launched and radioed ahead because I easily outran him. Just as Charles and I climbed in that '50 Ford to go home, we were approached by another fellow wearing a uniform. He pointed to the dock we had just left and asked, "Were you the one driving that speed boat?" I told him I was, expecting a compliment on my driving. "Then, you are under arrest!" he exclaimed. I looked him over good, saw no gun, and proceeded on my way. Two other uniformed fellows came running. One stood in front of the truck and another jumped on the running board of the driver's side. The fellow in front jumped out of the way when he saw that I wasn't going to stop while the other just held on commanding me to pull over. I must have been running about 30 mph and a quarter mile down the road when I yelled out the window, "Either you jump off this vehicle or I will knock you off!" To my surprise, he jumped off tumbling end over end.

"They're gonna lock us up," Charles calmly stated. I knew he was right, so I took us back to the trailer park as fast as possible.

Marie was cooking supper when I hooked that Zimmer to my truck. "What are you doing?" She insisted. I told her we were going home to the mountains. "You can't leave now! I've got supper cooking," she continued. To her objections, I dragged that travel trailer off the blocks and headed to Hayesville. I laid low at Pearl's for a couple of months hoping things would settle back down with the police department in Atlanta. While I laid low in Hayesville, Pearl and I started building our house there.

When funds were running low and I thought it safe to return to Atlanta, I moved Marie back to Atlanta again. I left the Zimmer at Pearl's and rented a house on Beaver Ruin Road. Judy was a baby and Leroy was on the way.

14-Older, But Not Wiser

I began to visit a small airport near Beaver Ruin Road. The manager was trying to sell an L-2, 1941 Taylor Craft plane. It would haul two people. I looked it over, not knowing much about planes. He wanted $1100 and would also take anything I had to trade. I made payments and traded him what I could until it was mine. The manager gave me a few flying lessons during that time. I even learned to take the old plane off. It smoked a good bit but seemed to run ok. Handing me the title, he told me that the plane was unsafe and that he wasn't going up in it again nor would he give me anymore lessons.

After pondering my dilemma over a week, I decided to fly the plane back to the mountains where I could fix it and practice. Sitting in that pilot's seat felt natural even though I had only a learner's license. I explained my plan to Fain, "We'll just slip down to the airport real early and take off before anyone gets there. You can help me navigate to Hayesville and then we will land in the field behind Uncle Jack Bristol's house." After quite a bit of persuasion, Fain reluctantly agreed to be my accomplice. At day-break the next morning, we arrived at the airport to initiate the plan.

When Fain saw my new plane he emphatically refused, "I am not getting in that death-trap!" I reminded him that he had to help me navigate to Hayesville. Fain taunted with rhetorical sarcasm, "Just how exactly do you plan to find your way home, follow the highway?"

I stated confidently, "Of course." It took a few minutes of begging but, I finally convinced Fain to stick to the plan.

After a few wobbly zig-zags, I managed to get that old Taylor craft in the air. From above, the roads in Atlanta looked like a big wagon wheel and I immediately lost my bearings. After a few minutes, Fain spied the dawning sunlight glinting off the golden dome of the Capital Building. I asked Fain, "Which road do we take outta here?"

He said, "I dunno, but I'm gettin' sick."

October 1962
Fain
Rex
My First Plane

I looked at the compass on the dash and reasoned aloud, "We live in North Georgia, don't we? Let's just fly north." I turned the plane and did my best to keep that compass on N. Shortly, we saw Lake Lanier, so we knew we were close to Gainesville.

We hadn't been in the air 15 minutes and Fain was already airsick and throwing up. As we flew across Lake Lanier he ordered, "Take me down as close as you can. I am going to jump! I'm probably a dead man, anyway!" I wasn't about to get close to the water because I knew he was serious.

I recognized an old feed mill from the air. I then knew exactly where we were because the highway to Hayesville went right by it. A few minutes later, I saw Brasstown Bald. It was easily recognized since it was the tallest mountain in Georgia and had a tower on top. By the way the crow flies, Brasstown Bald was only about 40 miles from Atlanta and 15 miles from Hayesville. I continued to follow the road through the Unicoi Gap headed to Hiawassee, GA.

I was feeling quite confident that we would reach our destination safely until we flew through Unicoi gap and the rising wind currents from the mountains began to toss us around like a rag doll. When the latch on the right side of the engine cowling popped loose and began to flail behind the prop, I began to worry that it might hit the prop on the front of the plane and cause us to crash. "Reach out there and latch that thing back down," I said to Fain.

He looked at me in astonishment and then calmly stated, "You think I'm crazy, don't you?"

I assured him, "Well you made it this far." Fain just shook his head as he unfastened the seatbelt and opened the door of the plane. He stretched as far as he could but lacked about two inches from being able to reach the latch. I still remember how the skin on his face flapped in the wind. "Give me your hand! I will hold you so you can reach the latch," I assured. Fain trusted me so much that as I held his hand, he stretched and managed to latch the cowling back down. I would have never let my brother fall, and he knew it. A few minutes later, we were flying over Hayesville.

I didn't tell Fain before we left Atlanta, but my few flying lessons had never included the landing part. I had decided that the best place to land would be behind Marie's Uncle Jack Bristol's house in a field owned by the Tiger family. I flew above the field behind Uncle Jack's house surveying the situation for about five minutes deciding how to attempt the landing. After I had planned my approach, I buzzed the cows to scare them from my chosen landing strip.

As I made my final approach to land the plane, I explained to Fain, "This might be a little bumpy. I have never landed a plane."

He angrily stared into my eyes in disbelief and yelled, "What kind of idiot are you? I can't believe you convinced me to take off with you!"

I calmly reassured, "Just hold on and pray. I will get you down safely."

I didn't realize at the time, but that field was too short for my first landing. I cut the throttle back and headed down just like the instructor had done in my few lessons. "Here we go, hold on!" I commanded. We hit the ground and bounced back into the air about 20 feet. Fortunately, after two or three bounces, I managed to get the airplane on the ground. The fence and highway were coming up quickly, and I was still going too fast.

Fain yelled, "Stop this thing!" I stood on the left pedal and the plane spun in two or three sliding circles and finally stopped.

"Whew, we made it!" I proudly reminded Fain. "Not bad for a first landing," I boasted. Fain was the first one out.

He fell face forward, kissed the ground, then stood and pointed at me, "Old buddy, if you fly this thing out of here, you will go without me. I am never getting back in a plane with you! You are crazy!" We left the aircraft in the field and caught a ride back to Atlanta.

I took the wings off the plane and hauled it to the house that we had built on Cherry Road across from Pearl and Margie's home. During the next few months, I repaired the aircraft, reassembled it in Frank Baumgarten's pasture behind the house, and then began to hone my flying skills. Over the years, I became an adept pilot. In fact, I flew that old restored plane many years before selling it. Quite some time passed before Fain boarded my aircraft again, but he did eventually come around after finally convincing himself that I did know how to operate the machine. Shoot, he even eventually parachuted from it as did many others. I flew for at least 25 years without a valid pilot's license. There weren't many Federal Aviation Agents in the area, so I didn't worry much about that. Eventually I did become a legal pilot.

Fain continued to live with me, Marie, and the kids as we traveled to and from our home in Atlanta to Hayesville. Like I said earlier, Fain was more like my son than my brother. During those years and our weekend visits to the mountains, Fain fell in love with Marie's younger sister, Roberta. They married when she was only sixteen. Eventually after my business had grown, I was able to support my family through the auto repair business I had established in Hayesville.

When we finally settled in Hayesville permanently, Fain worked alongside me in the shop. He and Roberta rented a small home in the Matheson Cove which was across the mountain from my garage and in the valley where Margie had grown up. Every day, Fain rode his Honda 90 across Cherry Mountain to work with me. Even though my business was growing, feeding two families on the meager income was tough. When Fain decided to move back to Atlanta to earn a better living, he had two children of his own, Mark and JJ. Jason was born later. Fain had evolved into a very great mechanic.

Fain was my best friend and I missed him sorely. Roberta and Marie missed each other too. Our families were together practically every weekend either in Hayesville or Lithonia, Georgia where Fain had settled with his family. We spent years camping together on Lake Chatuge or Fires Creek, picnicking and riding motorcycles on Cherry Mountain, or going to yard sales, auctions, and visiting outlet malls in Atlanta. Only the weekdays separated our families. Either way, we were always together on the weekends. Our children, double first cousins, grew up together. Weekends were the highlight of our lives.

Fain had won a nice console TV for two dollars at an auction in Lithonia, but the TV didn't work, as stated by the auctioneer. "I've fixed a few televisions in my time," he confidently remarked to me as he collected his prize, "and I can probably fix this one." Fain bragged about the beautiful woodwork on his new TV and repeatedly reminded me that he had gotten a real deal for two dollars.

It was almost 11 pm that same evening when Fain removed the metal plate from the rear of the TV, began to examine the diagram glued to it, and plugged the TV to the electrical outlet. The tubes lit up, but the screen was still black. He squatted to examine the internal structure, spit on his fingers, and started wiggling tubes to no avail. He decided that the problem must lie within the little silver transformer box sitting in the corner of the console. Fain carefully removed the silver metal cover, licked his fingers again and reached for its contents. A blue bolt of electricity leapt out of the box to his fingers before he even actually touched it, traveled through his body, and shot out his right ear to the metal back he had just removed. The diagram burst into flames.

Fain just fell back in the floor, yelling for Roberta. When she came running he commanded, "Open the <blankety-blank> door!" Fain crawled to his feet, grabbed the TV, and threw it into his front yard. Momentarily disappearing into his bedroom, he reappeared with his 30-30 rifle, walked to the TV and to our surprise, shot it three times. "Take that you <blankety-blank>! You'll never hurt anyone again!" Fain yelled. His actions reminded me of our Daddy in that moment, but he hadn't been drinking. Fain never attempted a TV repair after that evening and he wasn't a very good plumber, but he did become a fantastic automobile repairman. Although, he did have mishaps as an automobile mechanic.

As Fain grew older, his eyes weakened, and he began having trouble seeing detail. He must have been about 40 years old at the time. I had already resorted to wearing reading glasses as I worked on car repairs. One weekend, Fain was fussing about not being able to see. Giving him my quick fix, I told him, "Just go to Kmart and buy yourself some reading glasses." I should have, but didn't explain further. Fain heeded my advice.

When I saw him the next weekend, he was bragging on his new glasses. "Man, I can even see the hone marks in a cylinder!" He proudly declared. His glasses were entirely too strong. He looked as if he had cut the bottoms off two soda bottles. To his demise, Fain loved his new glasses so much that he began wearing them all the time.

A few weeks later, I went to visit him in Lithonia. He could barely walk and smelled strongly of Bengay arthritis cream. I inquired, "What in the world happened to you?"

He groaned, "I stepped off a car lift." I couldn't imagine how that could have possibly happened and pressed him for details.

Fain recounted, "I had raised a car on the lift and worked underneath it for a while. I needed to check the wiring under the dash. Since I was rushing to finish the job, I didn't take the time to lower the car. So, I just opened the passenger door and stood on a bucket and pulled myself in. I should have lowered that stupid car! Roscoe came by, asked a question, and then shut the passenger door. By the time I had finished under the dash, I had forgotten that the car was on the lift. I opened the driver's side and just stepped out. I was wearing my glasses, so I thought the floor was right there. I just stepped right off that lift like an idiot! That fall just about killed me!" I tried my best not to laugh, but I just couldn't help it. Fain was bruised and banged up a bit, but I knew he was okay. Fain continued, "I've been through four tubes of Bengay this week. Man, that's some good stuff. It gets pretty hot, though."

That was when Fain began his love affair with Bengay. He always kept a tube on the nightstand by his bed after that. It became his new cologne and always came up in our discussions. "Don't ever use Bengay on your feet!" He blindsided me with that comment one weekend. Puzzled, I just cocked my head and looked at him strangely. I had no words.

"I was going deer hunting last Saturday morning, went to kiss Roberta goodbye, and saw the Bengay on the night stand. I had the bright idea to use it on my feet to keep them warm. I grabbed the tube and rubbed my feet down real good before I left. My feet were sweating by the time I got to my tree stand. Man, that stuff got so hot that I had to wade the creek and it was 20 degrees outside. Don't ever put that stuff on your feet! They should really include a warning in the directions about that," he further cautioned. All I could do was laugh in disbelief at his misguided idea. Fain was my comic relief. He could always make me laugh.

15-Kids Will Be Kids

Poor Margie, I don't know how she survived those weekends when we all gathered at her house in Hayesville. I suppose she spent all week storing up prayers of protection for all the crazy people who would be on her property come Saturday. Margie owned the entire frontside of the mountain behind her home. Pearl had passed by then and Pat, Marie's third younger sister had married Ken Rogers. They had four children: Sandy, Kenny, Angela, and Patricia whom we nicknamed "Charlie." Jason, Fain's third son had been born and Susan, Marie's youngest sister, had married Cecil Dye and they had two children, Felisea and Chris. Uncle Bud, Marie's only brother, still lived at home and took care of the place. (See Appendix for photos.) Furthermore, many of our friends came over to take part in the gatherings. The group of family and friends had grown so large that we ate meals in the yard, porch or where ever we could find a place to sit. Margie truly did love her offspring because during that period in our lives, she let us have homecoming at her house almost every weekend. Many of our fondest memories were created there.

All of us boys had started riding trail bikes. Since Margie owned the entire mountain behind her house, we had trails and challenging climbs cut all over that mountainside. We older children spent the weekend days in manly competition to see who could climb the steepest trail while the grandchildren played in the nearby creeks and ponds. Margie's daughters just visited on the front porch and intermittently prepared meals for all of us kids. Margie was the cornerstone of it all. In fact, I don't think she ever even complained. Can you imagine having upwards of 50 people at your house every weekend riding

A typical Saturday at Granny's House

wildly on motorcycles, stripped-down cars, go-carts, bicycles, and anything else that had wheels? It was certainly quite the spectacle to say the least. Margie was one of the finest women I have ever met, and she certainly loved her family. She tolerated us virtually every weekend.

Buford and Mildred Ledford lived on Highway 69, about a mile from Margie's and my house on Cherry Road. Buford and Mildred were pastors at the Tusquittee Church of God at that time. Margie, of course, frequented that church. Ronnie their son, later told me that his mother had forbidden him from joining the crowd of law breakers on Cherry Road. "You can go watch from the ridge top," Mildred instructed, "But, you can't go down there." She knew that the whole bunch was wild and crazy. Mildred was afraid that her boy would end up hurt or in sin if he joined that rambunctious crowd on Cherry Road. Ronnie was a good boy, watched the excitement from afar, and later grew up to be a pastor himself.

I was friends with our two county state patrolmen, the sheriff, and all his deputies. They frequently visited my garage on Cherry Road, and I often took them fishing since I was the resident guide. Marie fed them lunch almost every day because they were trying to survive on a meager state salary. Besides, Marie had become one of the best cooks in the county. Seems I always had an officer eating at my table. I reckon they simply chose to stay away from Cherry Road on the weekends so they didn't have to arrest friends or their friends' children for riding on the highway unlawfully.

After the manly mountain climbing competition had ceased for the day, the kids took to the motorcycles that remained intact. Of course, our Honda 250s were much too big for all of them, but they learned to hang off the side to get started. Some of the kids were so small that we had to hold the bikes balanced while they took off and catch them when they tried to stop. The grandbabies looked like ants riding elephants on those grossly over-sized motorcycles. Nevertheless, the grandbabies all learned to ride like pros in Margie's yard and in the field across the road.

Inevitably, we always ended up drag racing motorcycles on the two-lane paved Cherry Road, both kids and adults. It was a short race from the top of Margie's hill to my mailbox about 150 yards away. That left sufficient time for all bikers to merge into one lane and stop in case a car rounded the curve about 50 yards past my drive. We carried on like that for years.

Margie had started raising guineas. For some reason, those guineas liked to hang out in the road just over the crest of the hill at Margie's driveway. Fain came across the hill one Saturday running about 70 mph only to see all the guineas in the road. He hit that flock of guineas and then the ditch. My goodness, Fain wrecked and tumbled all the way down the hill. Luckily, he didn't break any bones, but he and his bike were out of commission for a week.

Fain always did tend to exaggerate a bit and worried all the time. Whatever was in the forefront of his mind was the topic of the day's discussion. For weeks, he recounted his run-in with the guineas. Over and over he warned us, "Boys, I'm tellin' ya, those guineas are dangerous! They're the number one killers in the USA." We fell about the place when Fain first coined that phrase. In the weeks that ensued, He recounted his guinea story so often that Arlan finally painted a warning sign and posted it on the crest of the hill. "Warning! Guinea crossing, #1 killers in the USA!" Fain didn't think that sign was very funny, but the sign stayed there for years!

Dan Reid was one of my friends from Atlanta. He had been through a nasty divorce and was living with us at the time. One Saturday, he and Fain were drag racing with two other riders. They had pulled off and left the pack while nearing the finish line at my mailbox. While side-by-side, Dan glanced over his left shoulder and Fain peered over his right. Their bikes drifted together and collided about 40 yards from the finish line. Tumbling end over end, they both had a bad wreck. Dan had a broken arm and they both had terrible road rash. No one ever wore a helmet, and praise Jesus, no one died or got hurt severely. Seems we spent all week repairing motorcycles and letting our bodies mend so we could simply break them again the next weekend. We saw it all as great fun.

My first four children were stair-stepped in age; there wasn't more than two years between any of them. Maria and Judy were relatively calm little girls, they didn't get into much. Leroy and Teressa were something else altogether, because I never knew what mischief they would get into.

Maria always had a morbid side to her. She wanted to play funeral home all the time. In fact, she got quite good at conducting a funeral service, because anytime she found a dead critter, she forced her siblings to participate in the burial. Maria was the preacher, choir leader, and chief mourner. She could really conjure up a tear. When she cried, all the kids cried. It's kind of ironic that Maria now assists her daughter Wendy, who owns and operates her own funeral home in Atlanta.

Judy, bless her heart, just got lost in the mix. She was quiet and obedient. You never knew she was around. She was very creative and industrious. You know, the crafty type. She and her husband are very successful entrepreneurs. I never did worry about that Judy because she had a steady head on her shoulders.

Leroy and Teressa grew up playing together all the time. They were best friends and were always in competition with each other. I reckon daredevil was in their DNA. They were like Fain and me when we were kids, inseparable. Leroy was the chief schemer and mastermind, while Teressa bore the brunt of his failed experiments. I am certain that social services would have taken my kids had they known what I allowed them to do.

I had given the kids an old torn parachute. They took it to the laurel thicket below Margie's and built a playhouse by the creek. Both Marie and Margie supplied frying pans, food, and cooking supplies. They spent many summer days playing in that Laurel thicket just catching spring lizards, walking the fallen log, cooking, and having funeral services. Maria was nine or ten, so Teressa couldn't have been more than three.

The top of the pasture was between the laurel thicket and Margie's house. Pearl's old barn, the corn-crib, and shed were there too. Those out-buildings were also favorite play spots for the kids. The field was over-grown with multi-flora rose bushes, but the kids had made a trail from the laurel thicket to the barn. There had been an old saw mill about a quarter-mile up the mountain from the laurel thicket, but the only remaining traces were stacks of wood, slab piles and mounds of saw dust. The old saw mill was a snake den for copperheads and rattlesnakes. I had taught the kids to watch for snakes and which were dangerous.

As they made their way from the laurel thicket to the barn one day, they heard a baby bird chirping from under one of the big multi-flora rose bushes. Peering underneath the thorny branches, Leroy saw a baby bird that had fallen from its nest and scampered under the rose bush to rescue the helpless chick. Teressa followed and squatted beside him. As Leroy gently scooped up the baby bird to return it to the safety of the nest, a rattlesnake started singing. Leroy had been so taken with the baby bird that he had forgotten to check for snakes.

"We have to ease back out of here," Leroy whispered to his little sister, "Come on." Leroy eased out, but Teressa didn't follow. She just squatted frozen, gazing at the snake. Maria, Judy, and Leroy all failed to coax Teressa out of danger. I reckon she was frozen with fear. She wasn't more than three years old. Overcoming fear to rescue his sister, Leroy crawled back under the rosebush with that rattlesnake, took Teressa's little hand, and pulled her away from the path of danger. The kids continued to play in the laurel thicket and on Margie's farm, but always watched for snakes more carefully after that encounter.

Leroy and Teressa were always scheming and trying to build something out of nothing. If it had wheels, they would figure a way to ride it. One of my favorite memories is of watching them race a Tonka dump truck and a set of toy tractor wheels down our smooth, red-clay dirt driveway.

Leroy used a pillow from his Mama's couch to cushion his butt as he sat on the bed of the dump truck. Teressa rode the rear set of tractor wheels from a plastic toy tractor, long since broken. With two shop rags taped to her hands, she could steer those wheels anywhere by simply applying pressure to the wheels with her hands. When Leroy said go, Teressa balanced on those wheels, holding an L-seat pose, until she reached the bottom of the hill. Leroy balanced on the bed of the little Tonka truck.

No matter how hard he tried, Leroy rarely ever beat her to the bottom of the hill. Leroy tried to take the tractor wheels, but he couldn't balance them. In fact, Teressa was the only kid around who could ride her toy, so she never had to share. I reckon she had ninja skills that the rest of the kids didn't possess. It made Leroy crazy because his little sister beat him over and over to the bottom of the hill. They rode those make-shift vehicles until the driveway was smooth red clay from top to bottom. When it rained, Marie and I had to ride the ditch line with the car tires to get up the hill to the house because Leroy and Teressa had worn the driveway slick.

The little branch that flowed through Pearl's pasture originated on Cherry Mountain, ran through the laurel thicket, and then through a culvert on Cherry Road to join Blair Creek. The water was cold and clean providing a perfect habitat for trout. I hired Jack Shook to build a dam just in front of the culvert that ran underneath Cherry Road. When the pond filled, it was nine or ten feet deep at the dam and quickly became another favorite play spot for the kids during summer.

Maria and Judy were the life guards who watched over six-year-old Leroy and four-year-old Teressa any time they played at the pond without us being present. Leroy and Teressa had been forbidden from venturing to the pond alone since Leroy could only dog-paddle a bit, and Teressa couldn't yet swim. Leroy masterminded an avenue to skirt both issues: They just kept an extra pair of underwear hidden in the bushes at the pond so Marie would never suspect their swimming, and furthermore, Leroy had retrieved two plastic, gallon-sized Clorox jugs from Margie's trash to serve as floatation devices for Teressa. She simply held the handles of those capped jugs and paddled all over the pond. Everything went well until Leroy's sneaky streak manifested.

One day while Teressa was in the middle of the pond kicking around holding those white Clorox jugs, Leroy paddled up behind her and unscrewed the blue caps. Her jugs sank, and she did too. She recalled seeing the surface of the water about four feet over her head and hearing a small voice that said, "Just walk out." That's exactly what she did. Even at four, she remained calm and obeyed the voice. Leroy just thought that removing the lids was funny at the time, not realizing that she could have died that day. I know it was the voice of God who instructed and saved Teressa from drowning that day. I taught her to swim after that day and that small, still voice continued to speak to her.

Like I said, Margie was a good woman who loved Jesus and trusted Him to hear and respond to her prayers. She prayed all the time because it took a lot of praying to cover her extensive family. She knew we all needed a lot of prayers since her daughters had married wild men and were all raising wild children. Mine were the most adventurous of the lot and she witnessed the craziness of my kids virtually every day. Margie was like a second mother to my children because we lived so close by. Marie, Roberta, and Pat all had a deep faith, but since their husbands didn't go to church, they nor their children did either. That fact troubled Margie deeply.

Margie had gotten her driver license after Pearl died and took a job at Walter Fuller's sewing plant on Qualla Road in Hayesville. She dutifully worked all week to support Susan, her youngest daughter who still lived at home, and to buy gas for her blue maverick. I guess Margie was in her fifties by then.

Every Wednesday evening, Sunday morning and Sunday evening that blue Maverick became Margie's church bus. Taking matters into her own hands, she made her rounds picking up Pat's and my kids, packing them into that blue Maverick like sardines, and took them to church because we didn't.

Pat and Ken lived just across the Georgia line only four miles from her house. Fain and Roberta lived in Atlanta or I am sure she would have squeezed those kids in too. It was Margie who taught most of her grandchildren a deep faith in Jesus. I am grateful because they have needed and received many miracles in their lifetimes. I am also thankful for the church bus that took me to church. It was also as a small child that I had believed and prayed in mustard seed faith.

Margie spent countless hours with my children allowing them to work beside her in the garden, peeling apples, making pies, and preparing vegetables to can. She was never too busy for them, always making them feel important even though I am sure they were just in the way most of the time. She just put them to work, told Bible stories, and taught them gospel songs. Margie loved her grandbabies and pointed them to Jesus at every opportunity. Like I said, Margie was the cornerstone of the whole family.

Teressa especially loved Margie and spent more time with her than any of the other grandchildren. If a church service was being held anywhere in the area, Margie and Teressa were always there. Teressa got saved and baptized in the Holy Ghost at Buford and Mildred's church near the head of Tusquittee. It was Mildred who prayed with her. I didn't know what that meant at the time, but Margie sure did!

Margie and Teressa became best friends. When Teressa was older and Margie had retired, Teressa would get off the bus at Margie's and spend the evening with her watching *Days of Our Lives, Barnabas Collins,*

81

and *The Merv Griffin Show*. After supper, she left Margie's and came home to do her homework. They loved each other so much.

When Margie died many years later, Teressa had three sons of her own and was preaching in the largest church in Costa Rica while on a three-week mission trip there. She had visited Margie in the nursing home the day before she left and had already said her Earthly goodbyes. Teressa was preaching at the very moment that Margie died. Teressa's husband Stan contacted her by phone a few hours later and told her that Margie had died. "I know," she answered. "God had already told me that Granny would die while I was away. He left me with a choice to go or stay home. I chose to go, and therefore I must stay because that's what Granny would have wanted. She taught me to preach the Gospel, and I will. She's happy-dancing in Heaven and won't be at the funeral anyway! I told her good-bye before I left and that I would see her in Heaven. She will give us a tour when we get there." Teressa missed Margie's funeral but most of the family understood because they knew Margie very well. Jesus first, family next and well, everything else will fall in place. That was Margie's motto.

Well, back to the pond years earlier where Teressa almost drowned. Arlan lived with me by then and tinkered with me in the shop like Fain had. One slow day at the shop, he removed a gas tank from one of my junked cars and carried it to the pond. The tank made a perfect little boat for Leroy or Teressa, if the captain balanced well and kept the nozzle above the waterline. Periodically, they would paddle to shore with their stick oar and empty the water from the tank. A logical mind would wonder why the kids just didn't put the gas cap back on the tank to keep the water out. A mechanic, however, knows that the gas cap screws into the body of the car, not the tank itself. The caps wouldn't fit the tanks.

Finding great pleasure in their boats, Leroy and Teressa removed the gas tanks from every junked car on the hill. They had learned to use my tools, and I let them. I didn't care; I used the cars only for spare parts. I think they eventually had six or seven gas tanks in that pond. When all the cousins came over on Saturday to visit, they all had a boat. Shoot, they even built a 15-foot mud water slide down the red clay bank to the pond. It took a good three days for the red clay stains to fade from their skin after the weekend. My children were stained all summer. Oh, they had a time playing in that pond! I did too just watching them play and have fun. I tried to give them the peaceful

82

childhood that I never had. I reckon I lived my childhood through them.

On Saturday, Leroy, Teressa, Sandy, Kenny, Mark, JJ, and Angela roamed a mile radius around Margie's house. They marched single-file in that same order everywhere they went. Leroy was the commander in chief and brave schemer in the bunch. He wore an old Army helmet that Big-nose Ledford had given him. On Sunday, they went to church with Margie and then played. We never forced them to attend church, so in the summer, that was mostly Margie and Teressa.

It was a summer Saturday afternoon, and we had finished our trail bike riding. We were just visiting in the yard and sitting on the porch after having lunch. The kids began appearing one-by-one, sometimes in pairs on Margie's front porch. Out of breath, they all spoke of a big snake. The best we could figure was that Leroy was fighting a big snake up Blair Creek and the rest of the kids were with him. I didn't bother to check on them until Sandy showed up. She was high on the command chain. Only Leroy and Teressa were left. Dang, it was just a snake and Leroy was a snake charmer by then. I got on my motorcycle and went to check on them.

I met Teressa running for her life just down the side road leading to the field. Leroy wasn't far behind. About 30 yards beyond Leroy, I saw a black racer snake in hot pursuit with his head raised and hissing. That snake had chased the kids a good 100 yards. They had just surrendered the fight with it and run. Of course, it chased. I got off the motorcycle, placed it on the kick stand, grabbed a limb and headed toward the snake. It wanted no part of me, reversed and just crawled off. All I could say was, "That's one mean snake."

One day they cornered a big black snake in Margie's brooder house. Just as that snake darted through a big crack in the broken concrete floor, Leroy grabbed it by the tail. I reckon the snake wound itself around something under the concrete and a giant tug-of-war began. When Leroy grew tired of tugging, Teressa took over. They pulled on the tail of that snake until it died. It was well over six feet long.

Little Joe Dorsey was laying on a creeper working under his car in my garage. Leroy carried that snake to the shop and told Little Joe that Granny had sent him a present. When Little Joe asked what it was, Leroy threw that dead snake under the car with him. Joe hit his head so hard that he nearly knocked the car off the jack stands. When he finally got out from under the car, he had broken one of his front teeth. That was just mean. Leroy messed with Little Joe at every opportunity.

On Saturday night, *Shock Theater* and *The Twilight Zone* came on TV. Leroy and Teressa would stay late at Margie's and watch. The shows weren't over until eleven and then they had to walk home in the dark. Leroy helped make Teressa a track star by running off and leaving her every time. They would both come in just panting because they had sprinted over a quarter of a mile thinking that Dracula, Frankenstein, or a gargoyle was about to get them.

Leroy spent a lot of time making the cows chase them too. If you run, a cow will give chase. They had to walk about a quarter-mile through Max Waldroup's cow pasture to reach his old rock quarry pond. They fished over there about every day in the summer. Teressa was afraid of cows and for good reason. She was little, they were big and chased her any time she was with Leroy. Every day Leroy promised he wouldn't take off running, and every day he did. All one hundred of those Holstein cows would give chase. Leroy could still run faster than Teressa, so they were always right on her tail. They were harmless, but she didn't know that.

Leroy could out run Teressa until she reached ten. I had taken them to a Fourth of July field day in Murphy. Teressa had already chased down the greased pig. The footrace was next. The contestants had to run from the outfield fence, around home plate and then back. Even though they competed against much larger teenagers, she and Leroy quickly pulled off and left the pack. After they rounded home plate headed back, Teressa pulled up even with him and grinned. Leroy knew she was about to pass him and started shaking his fist at her. She just grinned again and fell in behind him. She let him win, and Leroy knew it. He couldn't beat her after that day.

The same thing happened when they started drag-racing motorcycles down Cherry Road. Leroy beat Teressa at first but after a few times, he just couldn't beat her. They would even swap motorcycles, and she still won. In fact, there wasn't a fellow around who could beat her. I used to get a big kick out of watching all the grown men get beat by my ten-year-old little girl.

I had an old red Sears & Roebuck motor scooter before I purchased my first trailbike. Leroy and Teressa rode that thing till it was worn out. Leroy was so small that he couldn't sit on the seat to steer, so he stood on the foot fenders. Teressa sat on the back and just held on. Eventually, it hung in second gear and the gas cable broke. That still didn't stop them. Leroy just fished the gas cable through the fender wall on the back. Teressa sat on the back with a rag and the gas cable wrapped around her hand. As she pulled the gas, Leroy steered. It smoked a good bit because they always rode wide open and really stressed the engine.

We lived on top of a big hill. It was steep in the front yard. I guess they must have made a million laps around the yard on that scooter because they wore the grass out that summer. I am not sure what possessed Leroy that day, but he headed the scooter toward the steep side of the hill in the front yard, looked at his little sister pulling the gas on the back, waved at her and said, "See ya'!" He just stepped off and sent her hurling off the side of the hill. She couldn't get off because she had the gas cable wrapped around her hand. She had a terrible crash. Nothing was broken, but Teressa got pretty banged up. That was the end of the scooter riding. She wouldn't get back on it, and Leroy couldn't ride it without her.

Leroy began riding my trailbike shortly thereafter. It was an XL100 Honda, completely too big for him, but he learned to crank it on the kickstand and hang off one side to take off. Like I said, if it had wheels, Leroy and Teressa could ride it. Leroy tied a tarp behind the motorcycle and Teressa rode it. They wore the yard completely out with that scheme. Later, I bought an XL250, an even bigger motorcycle, but they mastered that one just as quickly.

Leroy and Teressa had ridden a go-cart in the meadow between mine and Margie's house until the motor was completely spent. No worry. Leroy just tied the go-cart to the luggage rack on the XL 250 and Teressa rode behind. They had made a good quarter-mile track through the honeysuckle vines and had gotten so good that they could hit 50 mph in the straight parts of the field. I had big knobby tires on the motorcycle, so it really took a bite in the curves. Teressa drove like a professional race-car driver and Leroy looked like a motor-cross champion. They must have been about 10 and 8 years old. Like I said, they so reminded me of my childhood. I didn't drink, but I am sure they could have driven me to the liquor store.

I think it must have been Karma repaying Leroy for the day he sent Teressa off the side of the hill on that motor scooter. He swung wide in the curve at the end of the field and Teressa hit a pine sapling. She wasn't hurt, but when the rope pulled taut, Leroy was propelled over the handle bars of the motorcycle. He was buried under the honeysuckle vines. Teressa had to follow the moans and groans of her brother and ended up having to free him from the vines with a pocket-knife. He was banged up for a few days after that wreck.

In my late twenties, I enjoyed a short but productive career in drag racing. By this time, however, I had quit drag racing and taken up with dirt track racing again. Racing was my weekend job. Shoot, it was a second income because I was often in the prize money. Arlan was living with us then and helped me in the garage. He too had become quite an automobile mechanic. Since I was always in the process of repairing my race car, I had bought several junk cars to use for replacement parts. An old red Studebaker from my personal junkyard on the hill had already sacrificed its front fenders, hood, doors, and roof. It still had a good engine, interior, and the frame was still intact. I had purchased my own wrecker by then.

Upon my return from a fishing trip one day, I found that Arlan had pulled that stripped Studebaker out of the weeds, cranked it, and was teaching Leroy and Teressa how to drive in the field across from Margie's house. I didn't think too much about it and just smiled. Shoot, I was driving by age seven, too. Because they were so small, Arlan had retrieved two sleeping bags from the shed, taped them together, and had fashioned a makeshift booster seat so they could see over the dash of the car. Leroy and Teressa drove that Studebaker in the field all summer. Occasionally they rounded the curved of their racetrack in the field too quickly and ran into the creek bordering the field. When they did, Arlan or I just pulled the car out with the wrecker, cranked the engine again, and sent them on their way. Eventually, they began to drive that Studebaker on Cherry Road and across Cherry Mountain. I told them not to be on the paved road, but they didn't listen very well. They had, however, listened closely to my recounting of childhood memories of driving, Arlan included.

Business at my garage was slow the day Arlan got the bright idea to jump the creek in Frank Baumgartner's pasture about a half mile from my house. Arlan chose a spot at Blair creek where the water had washed deep banks directly in line with an old dirt road that led across the field. The locale afforded opportunity for a good fast start. To catch the car just in case the jump failed, Arlan dragged a few rotten pine saplings across the span of the creek banks. Arlan drove and Leroy rode shotgun. Despite Arlan's best laid plans, the front of the car cleared the far creek bank, but the rear end did not. They hit hard and that old Studebaker folded into an inverted V on the far side of the creek bank. After regaining his breath when the impact of the crash knocked the air from his lungs, Arlan made the short journey back to my garage, returned with the wrecker, and pulled the car to my shop for repair. I had taught him well because Arlan used a come-a-long to straighten the broken frame, welded I-beam rods on each side of the car to hold the frame together, and cranked it once again.

Studebaker made a tough vehicle. Leroy and Teressa continued to drive the car that summer even though the front wheels shimmied, and the rear end rhythmically swayed up and down when driven over 35 mph. Often, Maria and Judy sat on the rear end with their feet resting in the back seat to serve as counter weights that minimalized the vertical sway in the rear end. I decided to retire the Studebaker after Leroy and John Mark Cable, a teenaged playmate from Cherry Road, dead-centered an oak tree at the picnic ground near the house. Leroy suffered broken ribs as he sat in John Mark's lap driving when they hit.

There were six years between Merlin and  Teressa. Merlin was born September 12, 1968 and David on October 17, 1969. They were only 13 months apart. We figured that every kid needed a playmate. Merlin was sneaky and full of mischief like Leroy. Although David was bigger, Merlin aggravated the hound out of him. Poor Teressa, it was being tough or die as she grew up sandwiched between all those boys. They made her tough.

Merlin and David played together all the time like Leroy and Teressa had; however, they didn't get into near the trouble that Leroy and Teressa did. About the worst thing they ever did was set the hill on fire and burn up several vehicles for which I had to pay.

I had been trout fishing on Mill Creek in Towns County one day and was heading home. As I slowly drove the gravel road out of the refuge, a new born fawn began to chase my Bronco bleating at me. When I stopped, the fawn trotted up to me like I was its mother. It still bore its navel cord and the baby's mother lay dead in the ditch. Feeling sorry for the fawn, I loaded it in my Bronco and took it home to my wife. Marie had a special connection with animals and any other stray that found a way to her.

87

Marie feeding Bambi

Marie bottled fed that baby and it grew to become another member of the family. Bambi thought he was a kid. Every time Marie went to the store, she had to buy him candy like the rest of the kids or he would knock them down and steal theirs.

That buck was so tame that he followed Leroy and Teressa everywhere they went. Merlin and David sat on his back and played. They were both still in diapers. I had two red-bone hounds that guarded the deer and the kids. Bambi was a four-point

Rex feeding Bambi Hershey Chocolate Bar

the first year and a six-point the next. Marie made little fluorescent collars bearing his name so no one would shoot him.

David Marie Bambi

One day, Leroy and Teressa were walking down Highway 69 just past Granddaddy Cherry's old place headed to the Yellow Jacket Restaurant to get an ice cream. A man passed, slammed on his brakes, and came to a screeching stop. He jumped from his car and excitedly yelled, "Did you know you have a six-point buck following you?" They just looked at one another thinking that fellow must be a little touched in the head. They let him pet the deer and explained that Bambi followed them all the time. People came from far and wide to see and pet that tame deer.

Marie fed Bambi a biscuit while I sawed his horns off. He had scratched every vehicle around removing the velvet from his horns and was beginning to butt the children. He was only playing, but I became afraid that he would spear one of them. He disappeared a month or so later when deer season opened. The kids cried and cried when they found his

Merlin pulling Bambi's tail

collar in the field. All that remains of Bambi are home movies and photos of the kids sitting on his back playing with him.

We took in homeless animals and people our entire lives. The kids had pet fish, birds, mice, guinea pigs, squirrels, rabbits, skunks, opossums, dogs, cats, pigs, horses, cows, and deer. They never had a pet bear. I even tried to catch a baby moose once while on the Green River in Wyoming. Mama moose came out from under the surface of the water and almost caught me before I dove back into the Bronco.

About the worst stray I took in was an aged yellow lab. I picked him up while on a family picnic in the Smoky Mountains. It farted on us the entire two-hour journey home. It had a large growth on its foot and disappeared three days later. A few days after that, we began to smell rotting flesh in and around the house. That big dog had crawled under the foundation of the house and died. It was foul to say the least. I couldn't fit under the house and paid Maria two dollars to crawl under the house and tie a rope to it. The flesh was so deteriorated by then, that the rope pulled its hide loose. Maria had to crawl under there again and I had to give her two more dollars. I finally managed to pull it out. Whew, that was a nasty job.

16-Reconciliation

I would check on my Mama and Daddy periodically. I always found the same thing. Daddy was drunk, and Mama was just coping the best she could. She had never known much different anyway. Arlan, my baby brother, had been born just about the time we all left home, so he didn't really remember any of us. He grew up like an only child. Daddy didn't beat on him like he did us, but his life still wasn't good. They had finally left the old powerline house and moved into a house with electricity but still no indoor plumbing. Each time I left, I always gave Mama my phone number and urged her to call if she needed me. One day she called saying that she wanted to leave my Daddy and come back to the mountains. I told her to pack her bags and that I would be there to get her and Arlan the next day. Marie was pregnant with Merlin and Arlan had just entered the ninth grade.

We left early Friday morning heading for Belmont. I got pulled over on the way for speeding and the officer took my license on the spot. Marie had to drive. She did have a driver license by then, but had left them in the pocket of her shorts at home. She had ridden my motorcycle to town to get milk for the kids. I had told Marie stories about my family, but I don't think she ever really believed them until that Friday.

We arrived to find Daddy drunk in the yard. I introduced Marie and took her inside to meet Mama. Arlan was at school. I went outside to talk with Daddy. After a minute or two of small talk, he asked me to take him to get wine. "Alcohol is the love of your life, and I will take you to get some, but first we have to get Arlan," I informed. As Marie drove to Arlan's school, I watched Daddy in the rear-view mirror. He always carried a hawk-billed knife in his pocket and I always carried a 9mm pistol under the seat. He fished that knife from his pocket and I pulled my pistol. As he came at my throat with that knife, I caught his arm and stuck that pistol between his eyes. I reckon he knew I wouldn't shoot him, so he kept struggling trying to slit my throat. "Just keep driving," I assured Marie. I dropped the gun, punched my Daddy square in the eye again, and took his knife. "We're going to get Arlan from school. You will sign the papers. Arlan and Mama are coming to live with me in the mountains for a while until you can get control of yourself," I calmly stated. Daddy signed the papers, I bought him a case of wine, and headed to the mountains with Arlan and Mama. It took three weeks, but Daddy called begging Mama to come home. To my dismay, she wanted to go back to him, but Arlan didn't. He lived with me until he graduated high school and I took Mama back to Daddy's hell-hole as she desired.

Later, I went back to Belmont and brought them to the mountains for a visit. Daddy stayed sober for over a week. We visited his family, and he played with my children. He asked me to take him for liquor, and I refused. "I won't have that stuff around my children. It has ruined your family; it won't ruin mine," I firmly stated. He pondered my words and must have taken heed.

He called me shortly afterward and said "I want a new way of life. Move me back to the mountains." Leroy and I went to Belmont and brought them back to Hayesville. They rented a little house on Brasstown where Daddy got saved, joined a little church, and changed his evil ways. He became one of the humblest little men I have ever met. He studied the Bible every day. I allowed Leroy and Teressa to spend a lot of time with him because Daddy enjoyed their company. They did a lot of fishing in Brasstown Creek which was just across the ridge from his house. Daddy quickly realized that the pleasures in life had eluded him due to his drinking. God had truly transformed his life. I think I have managed to forgive Daddy for the things he did to our family as a child, but I don't think Fain ever could.

17-Someone Could Have Died

I've had many close calls in airplanes. Life taught me at a young age not to panic, but maintain a cool head in dangerous situations. It was that ability that saved me many times.

I returned home one evening from a trip to Colorado only to find my beloved 1941 Taylor Craft crashed in the field. Someone had decided to try to fly it and didn't do very well. The would-be pilot had run my plane through the barbed wire fence, busted the engine, and nearly ripped the wings off. It was beyond repair. I thought to myself, "What kind of idiot would try to fly a plane without knowing how?" I realized that I had done practically the same thing and dismissed the thought. I am pretty sure I knew who did it. Anyway, I bought a 1943, J3 Cub after that.

That yellow J3 had a seat in front and one directly behind. It was steered with a stick like a bulldozer rather than a steering wheel like a car. You could fly the plane from either seat, since it had two control sticks. It really flew too slowly for me. It was great for parachuting but not for aerobatics. I could loop it and do a snap roll, but that was about it.

At the time, I kept the plane in Richard Bristol's field on Tusquittee. The field wasn't very long, and I had to take off rather quickly to avoid the trees at the end of the field. The mountains were steep on both sides of the valley, but I had already been flying around the mountains of Clay County for years.

Fain had said he wanted to parachute from the plane. I had purchased a parachute and needed to make sure it would open and then learn to re-pack it correctly. I knew that I needed to practice the entire routine. I tied a case of C-rations to the harness, hooked it to a rip-cord and set it in the back seat of that old J3. After I took off and climbed to about 2000 feet, I would reach behind me over the second control panel, grab the chute, and toss it out my door. I had already given the chute two trial runs and everything had gone smoothly. I felt like I needed to do one more trial.

I re-packed the parachute, set it in the back seat and headed down the runway. I hit a big bump in the field, but the plane still lifted off just fine to clear the trees at the end. As I climbed, the plane drifted left. I tried to correct the plane's path, but the control stick wouldn't move. No matter how hard I tried, I couldn't budge that stick. I was still climbing but was heading straight for the mountainside. I realized that if I didn't do something fast, I would crash and likely die.

I had learned to keep a rational mind in a tense situation and knew I had to correct that left drift somehow and very quickly. I opened the door of the plane and started easing out the right-wing strut. Sure enough, the plane began to level off and fly straight. As I held on with the plane still climbing, I decided that when the plane climbed high enough, I would just get back in and use my parachute. Finally, the plane cleared the mountaintops and was high enough that I felt it safe to climb back in. Who would ever imagine it safer to hang on the wing strut of a pilotless plane than to be in the pilot's seat?

I had to be very creative that day. It was a few days later when I realized, "God answered the mustard seed prayer again." Oh, I cried like a baby when that revelation came. He had once again given a plan to survive and the courage to follow it.

When I climbed back inside the plane and reached for the parachute, I saw that it had bounced off the seat and lodged on top of the rear control stick. The plane was designed so that it could be piloted from either seat. That's why my front control stick wouldn't budge. I simply put the parachute back in the seat, hooked the seatbelt around it and then landed. I didn't feel like flying anymore that day after my brush with certain death.

Fain and many others safely parachuted from my planes, including my son Leroy and my daughter Judy. After Judy jumped and the wind blew her past her target into the trees, I never let anyone jump from my plane again.

Fain was up one weekend and wanted to take a ride in the plane with me. I took him up early the next morning. Lake Chatuge was so calm that it looked like glass. As I flew up the middle of the lake, I gently eased to the surface touching the wheels of the plane to the water. They slowly began to spin sending a spray of water upon the sides of the plane. After about 100 yards, Fain became a bit squeamish about the entire scenario and requested that I pull up. I did, but that was fun.

If the truth be known, ducks taught me more about flying than any one person. That J3 was slow, about duck speed. I would fall in with a flock of ducks and just fly among them. If they dove, I dove. When they veered, I veered. I traumatized the geese and ducks on Lake

Chatuge, but I learned to fly with them and to gently feather the controls.

Little Joe Dorsey was one of my best friends. He had married Betty Nicely. She was from a family that lived on Coker Road off Myers Chapel. Our families spent a lot of time together and Stella, Betty's mother worked for Uncle Jack Bristol as a housekeeper. The Dorseys and Nicelys were some of the nicest people I had ever met. Our kids played together, spent the night with one another, and we picnicked all the time. Stella was quite the cook.

Little Joe came over to my shop one morning and informed me that he had decided to finally take a ride with me in the airplane. He had never flown before. I needed a break anyway, since I had been working all morning. The beauty of being self-employed was that I could stop anytime I wanted. I dropped my tools and off we went. We drove to Tusquittee and boarded that old J3.

"You ain't gonna cut no die-doves, are you?" he asked as we taxied down the grass airstrip. I assured him that I would just take him for a nice ride. 'Nice ride' seemed to be relative to the speaker. I had flown over his house, pointed to landmarks on the ground, and had given him a very nice guided tour of Clay County from the air. He had relaxed and was truly enjoying the ride when I spied a flock of ducks flying over Lake Chatuge. I forgot about Little Joe sitting in the back seat.

I was like a dog chasing a squirrel as I flew amidst my duck friends. I darted left and right diving with the ducks even doing a few snap-rolls before I remembered my passenger. I peered over my shoulder to make eye-contact noticing that Little Joe had his arms threaded through the frame bars and his feet latched around the seat. He was holding on for dear life! My black friend was pale as a ghost. "What's the matter with you?" I asked.

"Man, I 'bout fell out of this thing back there with you chasing them ducks!" I looked at his waist and saw that he wasn't wearing his seatbelt. The doors on that old J3 would open if you pushed on them, so I didn't doubt his word.

"You're not wearing your seatbelt!" I exclaimed.

"This thing has a seatbelt?" he puzzled. Poor Little Joe, I almost dumped him from my plane without a parachute. After that incident, I learned to make sure my passengers were buckled in safely before leaving the ground.

I sold the J3 Cub and bought a 1946 BC-12-D Taylor Craft. I absolutely loved that plane. I could take off and land it practically anywhere, even in knee-deep weeds. Making a stall landing, I could set it down and stop in 50 feet and even land it on one wheel. That's the plane I flew under the catwalk on Lake Chatuge when the lake was full. I even landed that plane on the dam. I flew it around here for at least 25 years teaching myself to do all kinds of aerobatics and stunts. That aircraft was like an extension of my body; however, I did have several mishaps in it.

Shortly after I had purchased the plane and felt comfortable flying it, I asked one of the instructors at the Andrews airport how to do a spin. He refused to disclose the information and furthered that the maneuver was too dangerous. Well, I had watched him do spins. Thinking he was being a bit hypocritical, I vowed to teach myself.

On my first attempt at a spin, I took the plane up 2000 feet, put it in a dive, and turned the aileron to the right. The plane began to spin but redlined before I had completed the first full twist. The redline on the airspeed indicator was the warning zone at which the plane might begin to break apart. I quickly decided that was an incorrect way to complete the maneuver and pulled the plane out of the spin. After a bit of pondering, it occurred to me that I should fall into the spin stalling the plane first. I put the plane into such a steep climb that it was about to fall from the sky tail first, and then fell forward into the same dive. That procedure worked like a charm. I kept playing until I got good at spins.

We have a lot of foggy mornings in these mountains. A thick fog tends to settle in the valleys leaving the mountaintops completely clear. GPS didn't exist when I was flying in those days, and I flew by sight or by charting a course using compass headings and a map. I knew a 50-mile radius of Clay County like the back of my hand. Even if I couldn't see the ground, I knew exactly where I was by recognizing the mountains. It was never safe to try to fly in the fog and I rarely did but I pushed my luck this day.

I had taken off and landed on the airstrip in a field at the house so often, I could practically do so with my eyes closed. Well, at least I could take off. I needed to go to Gainesville, GA to obtain car parts for an urgent vehicle repair I had taken under contract. Marie decided to go with me that day. The kids were at school and Gainesville was only about a 20-minute flight from my house. We could be down there and back very quickly.

The fog was especially thick that morning. I was low on fuel but knew I had enough to fly to Gainesville and I would just fuel there. Marie totally trusted me, so I took off from the field with little to no visibility. I saw a little blue sky through a hole in the fog and headed for the hole to get above the fog. They call those sucker-holes for a reason. Sure enough, it was clear as a crystal above the fog and we headed to Gainesville Airport.

When I flew across Brasstown Bald, I saw ground fog in all directions as far as I could see. I had flown into the Gainesville airport often and knew about how long it would take and where it was from the air. I wasn't more than eight minutes away. It was then that I realized we were in trouble. I radioed the air-controller in Gainesville and asked about the conditions. He said, "We are totally socked in. In fact, all the airports from here to Macon are." I felt fear grip my very soul because I knew we were low on fuel. When Marie heard the controller, she glanced at the fuel gauge, came to the same realization, and began to pray. I started looking for a sucker-hole in the fog because I was going to at least try to land somewhere. I flipped to the reserve tank and kept circling the spot where I thought the airport should be while knowing we were almost out of fuel. I had informed the air-controller of the situation and that I had to land somewhere. When the engine sputtered the first time, all of a sudden a sucker-hole opened and I shot through it. Low and behold, it was over the airport. I landed and as I taxied to the gas pumps, the engine died.

"This was stupid!" Marie said as she looked at me with tear filled eyes. I couldn't argue because I knew she was right.

I finished my business in Gainesville and the fog lifted. We made it home before the kids got off the school bus that evening, but we decided that we shouldn't fly together again until the children were grown. Merlin and David were born after that incident, so it was many years before Marie flew with me again. If I had crashed that day, someone else would have raised our four children. I believe that God took His finger, stirred the fog, and opened that sucker hole over the airport to preserve our lives that day.

Years later, I was giving Merlin flying lessons. Since he had his pilot's license at 14, he must have been 12 or 13 years old at the time. That plane didn't have a radio to contact the controller at the airport.

To earn his pilot's license and make his solo flight, Merlin had to communicate with the air traffic controller. It just so happened that I had purchased and installed one the day prior to the following occurrence. I had simply connected the radio to a lawnmower battery that I sat in the floor of the plane. I didn't secure the battery. It was another one of those foggy mountain mornings and I had never attempted to fly in the fog since that near-death experience at the Gainesville Airport many years earlier.

Merlin and I were sitting in the plane listening to the radio and talking about flying. I was just teaching him about the plane and talking with him about the instruments. A voice came over the radio calling for the controller at Andrews Airport. "I think I am circling Andrews and I am very low on fuel. I can't find the airport." The pilot said, "I am circling the tower on the mountain. Help me get down," he continued. I knew there was no tower on the mountains at Andrews and that the pilot wasn't in Andrews. He was lost and low on fuel. I figured that the pilot was circling the tower on the top of Brasstown Bald. The controller shortly communicated that very fact.

I picked up the microphone on the radio and instructed the distressed pilot, "Keep circling the tower, I am coming for you."

I knew what it was like to be low on fuel and lost. I also knew that what I was about to do was just stupid. I was compelled to help that fellow so, I cranked the plane and took off from the pasture through the thick fog. Like I said, I knew the mountains of the area like the back of my hand, and I had taken off and landed in the little grass strip so often that I could have probably done so with my eyes closed.

As I ascended, I looked at Merlin and said, "Never, ever do this!" The fog was thick, 300 to 400 feet deep. I emerged above the fog and headed to Brasstown Bald. It only took about five minutes for me to locate him. Sure enough, he was circling just where I thought. "I've got you in my sights!" I told the lost pilot. "Can you see me?" I questioned. In a few seconds, he responded that he could. "Ok. Fall in behind me. I am going to take you to the airport in Andrews and help get you down. It's not more than 12 minutes away," I instructed.

"That's good! Because I don't have more than 15 minutes of fuel left!" He replied. He fell in right behind me.

As I flew across Tusquittee Bald, I could see that the valley in Andrews was totally covered by a blanket of fog too, and that landing was going to be treacherous. I knew that valley very well. It was wide and long and even if we did miss the airport, I could land in the fields if necessary. I only hoped that he could too.

"I am going to fly to Topton, locate the highway, and bring you into the airport. Whatever you do, just keep me in sight. I may have to pull up, but just follow me!" I instructed the pilot of the other plane.

I found the road on the top of the mountain at Topton and headed toward the airport. I descended when I thought the time felt right, and he dutifully followed. I flew through the fog looking for the airstrip. Visibility was limited to about 200 feet. I saw it and he ensued. We both landed safely.

We taxied back up the runway and the air-controller/manager met me. "You've done your good deed for the day! That was very brave and very stupid," he congratulated. We were friends, and I knew he was right. I was just very relieved that we were on the ground and agreed. I held back my tears, though not as I write, when the pilot and his small daughter exited their plane. She couldn't have been more than four. I had just assumed he was alone, since he never mentioned a passenger. Honestly, I don't know if I could have done what I did had I known that a baby was aboard. God had prepared me for that day. I never flew in the fog like that again, but I did find myself trapped in a snow storm.

When engaging in aerobatics in an airplane, any unsecured object tends to float about the plane. I let my children experience zero gravity as I maneuvered from a stall to a slight dive. I simply let them unfasten their seat belts and float about the cab like astronauts. They loved it.

It was a week after the fog rescue had taken place, and I had completely forgotten about the battery left sitting unsecured in the floor of my airplane. I had been busy with the normal events of life and had not taken the time to fly my plane. At that point in my flying career, I had added loops to my list of aerobatic maneuvers. It was just stupid of me to leave an unsecured object in the plane, especially something the size and weight of that lawnmower battery.

I had flown all about Clay County relieving stress and enjoying my ride. All was well until I decided to make a loop. I put the plane in a steep climb and just when I reached the peak of the loop, that battery flew from the floor of the cab, across the back of the seat, and fell to the tail-section of the plane. The battery fouled in the control cables, and I couldn't steer. Instead of completing the loop, the plane began to fall tail first out of the air. I can only surmise that the elevator caught so much wind that the plane felt as though it had stopped in mid-air. The plane then did a whip-stall all by itself. When it did, the battery fell back to the front of the plane hitting the back of my seat and freeing the steering mechanisms. After I regained control of the plane, I began to smell exhaust strongly. I decided to land at the Andrews airport so the mechanic could have a look. That battery had fallen through the bottom of the plane ripping a huge hole in the fabric. How could I have been so stupid? That old gruff mechanic fussed at me good and patched the hole. He said, "You need to bury this old plane. The fabric is rotten and you're going to get killed in it!" I had learned my lesson that day: It's important not to have loose objects in a plane, especially people and batteries. Another hard lesson followed shortly thereafter.

We had established a routine. I would buzz the house barely missing the tree tops as a signal that the show was about to begin. Marie and the kids would all run outside in the yard to watch. After flying beside the hill a couple of times to exchange waves at eye-level, I would climb high and give them an aerobatic performance. We had gone through the routine several times when, as the kids watched one day, that old plane wouldn't pull out of a spin. I fought the controls for all I was worth and finally managed to pull out of the spin about 500 feet above the ground. The plane wasn't flying right, so I knew something was wrong. The kids thought I was just being exceptionally brave that day. I flew it on to Tusquittee and landed.

After looking the plane over good, I couldn't find anything wrong. I finally climbed up on the wheel to look at the top of the wings only to discover that three full sections of fabric were missing from the left wing. Lesson learned. That old mechanic was right. I drove back to the house, got one of Marie's bed sheets and taped it over the holes in the wing. I flew the plane straight to Andrews and hired them to recover the wings with new fabric. It would have been an awful thing for my children and wife to have watched me crash right before their eyes. I got better at recognizing danger after that incident, but sometimes I just had to embrace it.

I had to fly my plane to the airport in Hendersonville to have something serviced that the mechanic in Andrews couldn't handle. Hendersonville wasn't far from Asheville and the Asheville airport had radar since commercial flights flew in and out of that facility. Hendersonville was about 100 miles from Hayesville, about a 45-minute flight. It was winter.

On the flight out, I saw thick clouds before me. No big deal, you just fly through the clouds and pop out on the other side. I didn't know it at the time, but it wasn't simply a thick cloud. It was the edge of a storm front moving into the area. The snow was thick and heavy. I simply held my course, flew out of it, and landed in Hendersonville. Flying in snow is like flying in fog. You simply can't see.

The mechanic informed me that it would be a few days before he could fix my plane. I found myself stuck in Hendersonville without a ride back to Hayesville which was two and a half hours away by land. I was about to call Marie to come get me when Dr. Size landed in a brand-new plane to refuel. He had just purchased it and was headed home to the Andrews Airport. I had seen him taking flying lessons there and figured I could just hitch a ride. That way, Marie could get me in Andrews. He agreed to take me along.

I told him that I had flown through heavy snow on the way out and that he might want to wait around and see what the weather was going to do. He said, "I really need to get home. If you are going with me, get in. We'll go up and take a look. If it's bad, we will turn back and land." I figured that since he had that brand-new fancy plane, he knew what he was doing and climbed in with him. He didn't even check the weather forecast.

We hadn't been in the air ten minutes until he flew straight into that storm. New pilots tend to over steer when they can't see, and that's exactly what he began to do. I had learned by experience that when visibility is limited, the pilot must make very subtle movements. I started watching the altimeter and knew he was flying too low to safely cross the mountains that lie between Hendersonville and Andrews. I tried to convince him to go higher and he just kept fighting with the controls veering left and right but yet not climbing higher. We were lost.

Through the snow, I caught a glimpse of the trees on a mountain and I knew we were about to crash. I grabbed the controls on my side of the plane and yelled, "Let go!" I took over the plane and immediately climbed as fast as the plane would without stalling. I reached 7000 feet and held the plane steady. The highest peak in Western North Carolina was just under that, so I figured we were safe at that altitude. We were lost in the snow but above the tallest mountain. Fortunately, we had a full tank of gas. Doc Size was shaking like a leaf.

100

"You can take back over now," I told him.

"I can't fly this plane in this storm, and I am lost," he said. I assured him that I was, too. "You have to take over, Rex. I only have 17 hours flying time and I can't do this," he continued. Neither of us knew if we were flying into the storm or out of the storm. I took over as he requested.

I knew the situation was not good, got on the radio, and called for the tower at Asheville. I knew they had a radar screen and could possibly detect our plane if we were nearby. The controller gave me two headings to take one after another that would produce a zig-zag pattern on the radar. Sure enough, he picked us up on the screen. After a few tense minutes of following exact headings, we flew out of the storm and the controller led us back to the Hendersonville airport. I landed the plane safely. We waited out the storm and then flew back to Andrews late that evening.

A couple of weeks later, I received a letter in the mail asking for my pilot's license. Apparently, they were convinced that I had been the pilot of the plane. They insisted that I should have informed them over the radio that I was taking control of the aircraft. Shoot, all I had was a student permit issued before my first flight with Fain. I tried to explain the details of the incident, but the FAA didn't care. So, I mailed them my 1958 student license. That was the best I could do since I had been flying for over 30 years on a student's license.

During that year, I took official classes with Bob Hendrix and obtained my full pilot's license with instrument and commercial certifications. That is, I became a legal pilot and could officially haul passengers. Unfortunately, Doctor Size crashed on Tusquittee Bald a few years later killing himself and the father of twin brothers. The twins survived the crash fortunately. Injured and bleeding, they walked many miles over rough Fires Creek terrain before they were rescued. It was my son Merlin who located the downed aircraft after scouring the mountainsides of Clay County from the air. Continuing my studies, I earned an aircraft mechanic certification, took a job at Andrews Airport, and worked there until finally retiring at 75.

I guess the scariest near miss was when I landed my Taylor Craft in the field beside Tom Day's house. Merlin and David were about three and four years old. I had both in the plane with me while Teressa watched from the ground. The front wheels were held in place by bungee cords about a half-inch in diameter. Just as I took off that evening, the bungee cord on the right wheel broke. I flew around for a few minutes while formulating a plan to land. I didn't tell the boys what was happening because I knew they would get scared. I knew a crash was unavoidable.

I had learned to land on one wheel. As I landed, I put the plane almost in a full stall and brought it down on the left wheel. Before it stopped completely, that right wheel collapsed, the prop hit the ground, and the plane tilted forward on its nose. Gas began running from the wing tanks, but it didn't flip over. I knew we were safe, so I climbed out, pulled the tail back down, and safely retrieved the boys. I fixed the plane, had it running again a few days later, and once again thanked God for preparing me for that day by teaching me to land on one wheel. Crashing with two of my kids beside me and another just watching was a tough path to walk.

My last plane and the one I crashed with Merlin and David.

18-Pushing the Limits

In retrospect, I suppose I tested the limits of societal graces with some of my antics. I never meant to cause harm or hurt anyone, I simply liked to help folks solve problems and make them belly laugh. Nothing pleased me more than making a child smile, bringing happiness to a sad heart, or helping to calm a worried mind. However, I must admit that I did draw devious pleasure helping braggarts regain a healthy perspective about themselves.

For many years, the superintendents of Clay County Schools allowed me to give the students an end-of-year airshow. After the teachers had assembled the students in the stands of the football stadium, I did my best aerobatics for them. For the grand finale, I flew low over the field and dropped a bushel of candy. An attached parachute always landed their treat safely on the turf. I loved watching the kids all run onto the field to partake of the candy. Most of the students had rarely ventured outside Clay County, so my annual show brought them a bit of excitement. I continued that practice for years until it was deemed too dangerous to continue. I never really saw dropping a candy parachute as dangerous, but I suppose it was. Luckily, the stunt always went off without complication. I would be put in prison for such now-a-days.

Hartsel Moore was the Sheriff of Clay County for many years. We were friends. Vehicles were still allowed to drive across Chatuge Dam at the time, but it still hadn't been paved. Folks used to camp at the far end of the dam. One summer, a bunch of hippies and young folks set up camp on the dam and had been hosting a 24-hour party there for weeks. Hartsel had tried every trick he knew to run them off but had failed. They weren't really breaking the law by being there and they knew it. They refused to leave. He rode out by the shop one morning and was fussing about the situation. I listened and told him that I could get rid of them for him. "What makes you think you can make them leave when I can't?" he questioned. I confidently reassured him again that I could make them leave. Hartsel said, "Just don't hurt them."

After a bit of pondering, I formulated a plan that I felt sure would be successful. Vaughn Gibson was family. His father and my grandmother were brother and sister. Vaughn had chicken houses. He used to sell eggs from his house on the corner between the school and Johnny Beal's old store which is now the Best Little Ice Cream Shop in Hayesville. I went to Vaughn's chicken house and filled ten plastic bags with the rawest chicken manure I could find. Wow, it was rank. I put my stink bombs in a 5-gallon bucket and carried them to my plane just before dusk that evening. I surmised that the party would be getting lively by then. When I made my first pass, it was evident that the party was hopping since the attendants' cars covered over half of the dam. They had all congregated in the woods on the far end. (That location would be in the right corner of the photo below, and the catwalk is the metal walkway that leads to the concrete structure in the midst of the lake.)

Photo Courtesy of www.tva.gov   Built for the People: **Chatuge Dam**

Removing the doors from the plane gave me a clearer view of the situation. After several low fly-bys to get their attention, many of the young folks and hippies ran out on the dam waving and smiling at me. I just waved and smiled back. I flew so low beside them that they could almost read the time from my watch. I flew under the cat walk and then touched my wheels to the water. By then, I had lured almost every one of them out of the woods. That was most certainly a big crowd, and I was staged to launch my air assault.

On the next pass, I flew above the center of the dam road and dropped a bag of manure on the people near the cat walk. It landed right in the middle of the crowd. Immediately, they began scrambling down the rocks headed for the lake. On the next pass, the main hippie stood with arms wide open. I imagined that he thought that I was making a drug drop. After all, my bags were filled with green, organic material. Bull's eye, that bag hit him right in the chest and splattered in all directions. After I had dispensed all ten bags on the crowd, the lake was full of hippies. Before I flew away, the dam was one stinky place full of a bunch of drunken and bewildered hippies and teenagers.

Hartsel came out to see me the next morning and told me there wasn't a hippie left at the dam. "Man, that place smelled awful and there was chicken manure splattered everywhere! Did you do that?" He inquired.

I didn't say anything but, "Well good...problem solved." I assured him that I didn't hurt anyone, but it might take a few days for the smell to go away.

Lonnie was Eual's boy and my first cousin. He came off as being just a gruff Command Master-Sargent, but Lonnie had a heart of gold. Lonnie and Evelyn helped us a lot when we were first married, and we visited one another throughout the years. He and his wife Evelyn had been up to visit, and I took him all around the area and gave him a guided tour from the air. Lonnie decided that Clay County would be a wonderful place to conduct maneuvers. That was a two-week training exercise for the troops.

The next summer, Lonnie brought his troops to the mountains to train. The troops housed at the VFW building and landed their helicopter on the ball field. They gave free rides to the public. I landed my plane in the cow pasture behind the softball field that has now been converted to little-league baseball fields. I had great fun during that two-week training session, took many of the troops for rides, and made a lot of new friends.

After several of the soldiers had taken rides with me, one who had remained watching from the ground said, "Where I come from, they really know how to fly. My instructor can land his plane with the engine cut off." I told him I thought I could do that too. Well, I knew I could do that, because I already had. "I've never known anyone else to land with no engine," he continued. I gave a few more rides, and he finally decided to take a ride with me.

I took the plane up to 2000 feet and killed the engine. "Hey man! What are you doing?" he exclaimed. I reminded him that he had said his instructor had landed with no engine and told him I thought I should try it. I glided down and landed in the field again. We stopped short of the normal spot, so I climbed out, turned the prop, and started the engine. Rather than taxi on to drop him off, I just took off once more.

"Where are you going?" he asked. I told him that I hadn't really given him much of a ride and flew towards the dam. I knew that some of his fellow troops were repelling off the cat walk. I decided that he needed to fly under the cat walk.

The lake was completely full, and I did realize that I would have to fly and judge perfectly to execute such a dangerous maneuver. I decided I could clear the water. That young soldier guessed I was about to fly under the cat walk and got down in the floor board of the plane, begging me not to. Yes, it was mean, but I flew under it anyway. After that, I took him back to the VFW. He was glad to get out of the plane and exited with a silent humility.

Shortly thereafter, he and one of his buddies returned to Hayesville to take flying lessons with me. I did teach them, and they gave me C-rations or whatever they had saved from their extra army supplies as pay. They must have thought I was an instructor, but all I had was a learner's permit. I had flown around Hayesville for 25 years without a bona fide flying license. I had taught myself a lot of the dos and don'ts of flying during that time.

I even took Captain Beckwith for a ride during that two-week period. He was a huge man and his feet looked like sleds. He and Lonnie sat at our table fighting the children's forks as they reached for a piece of Marie's fried chicken. He later became a colonel and was famous for a failed mission to rescue American hostages in Iran. I think their plane became buried in the sand or something. He was a fine fellow. I continued to visit him and Lonnie at Fort Bragg at every opportunity.

On my way back from Fort Bragg after a visit, my plane began to run low on fuel. I had enough gas to make it to Franklin and would just refuel there. At that time, I still flew using a map and headings. Convinced I had reached Highlands, I just tossed the map, since I thought that I was in my own neighborhood. Shooting around what I thought was a familiar mountain, I saw an unfamiliar rocky-faced mountain before me. Shocked at the realization I was lost and running low on fuel again, fear tried to grip me. I calmed myself knowing that God knew exactly where I was and that He would provide a way of escape from my predicament.

God granted me courage and steadied my mind. He led me to begin the search for a place to land. I saw a fellow plowing in a field below and just landed my plane in his field. I climbed out of my aircraft and asked that farmer where I was. "You mean to tell me that you don't know where you are?" he calmly asked. I assured him that I was lost. "You are in Tamassee, South Carolina," he informed. I had never even heard of the place. I thanked him and returned to my plane. I looked at my chart and sure enough found Tamassee. I was about 40 miles off course. I charted a course to Franklin, refueled and flew on home.

Another time, when Leroy was a tyke, he had flown with me to Fort Bragg. Since Cramerton was on the path back home to Hayesville, I decided to stop off and visit Mom and Dad for a while. I landed in a field about 2 miles away from their home and then caught a ride to their house. I heard sirens running up and down the road but didn't think much of it. After we visited with Mom and Dad, I took off from the field and flew to Belmont to refuel. One of the employees at the airport asked if I had seen a crashed plane. I told him that I hadn't.

A couple of weeks later, I received a newspaper clipping from Mama that included an article about a missing pilot and a picture of my plane. I had caused quite a stir with my short visit with Mom and Dad realizing that I had evoked the sirens I heard passing near their home. I reckon the air traffic controllers at Douglas Municipal had lost my plane from radar. I had landed in the field, but they assumed I had crashed. I never meant to cause problems. Like I said, I was a bit backward when it came to social graces.

I had discovered that if I stalled my airplane and put it in a spin, it had enough wind speed at 110 mph to crank itself again. Lloyd Young and one of his friends had asked me to take them to an airport in Tennessee to inspect an airplane for possible purchase. On the way back his friend asked, "What would you do if the engine just quit?" Being close to the airport, I knew I could land if the engine didn't crank. I just turned the engine off. "What are you doing?" the friend exclaimed. I put the plane in a dive and sure enough, it cranked itself at 110 mph. When the prop started spinning again, he had the answer. After we landed, he looked at Lloyd and said, "If I ever start to open my mouth with a stupid question like that again, just slap me."

19-Jesus Take the Wheel

I was diagnosed with melanoma in the tissues around my right eye about 15 years ago. After surgery to remove the cancer four different times, I bore deep scars and lost the tear duct. With each surgery, my vision decreased until I finally lost sight in my right eye completely. My doctor told me that I had to resort to radiation treatments and wanted to remove my right eye. I refuse to let him remove my eye because I never got peace about that, but I did make the decision to take the treatments. Those cancer treatments were tough, but I whipped it. I didn't have to slow my pace too much. I had a green light in my spirit to fight. Cancer is a formidable foe, but I squared off with my Goliath.

I found myself laboring for breath just doing small chores. I wasn't used to that. I had always been able to do what I wanted, when I wanted, for as long as I wanted to do it. That bothered me and cramped my lifestyle. Marie pestered me about it until I went to see Shirley Youngblood. After running a battery of tests, Shirley referred me to Doc Kelley, a renowned heart surgeon whose primary practice was in Atlanta. He had opened a practice in Hiawassee, and later in Blairsville so that he could offer his expertise to our area. He resided in Young Harris, a small town located between Hiawassee and Blairsville. In my opinion, there's a lot to be said about people who return to say thanks to those who helped them on their way to success. Doc Kelley has prolonged the lives of a lot of folks in this area. These old mountains have produced some of the most brilliant minds that have ever lived. Oh yeah, Doc Kelley's children are famous too. I mean really famous! Charles sings with Lady Antebellum while Josh cut top albums and married Katherine Heigl, a popular actress.

Well, I knew Doc Kelley as a small boy and teenager. I had fixed his stranded vehicle several times, and he was also Charles Burdette's step-brother. Remember, Charles lived with us in the 30-foot Zimmer when we rented the speed boat at Lake Lanier. We narrowly escaped prison over that incident. Luckily, Doc Kelley was never with us when we got into trouble or he likely would have never been called Doctor. I trusted him.

Whatever Doc told me to do, I did unless it included drastic lifestyle changes like giving up sausage gravy and biscuits. I decided that I should just enjoy the years I had left. Long story short, Doc Kelley and his partners kept unclogging the pipes in my neck and added many years to my life. I am grateful for his wisdom and willingness to help out an old country boy. Doc Kelley never forgot my rescuing his stranded vehicle, so he repaired mine over and over. I fixed broken trucks and he fixed broken circulatory systems. I felt like a million dollars for a while every time stents were replaced. When I was feeling exhausted again and my stents weren't blocked, Doc told me that my heart muscle was hardening and there wasn't anything he could do about that. He gave me medicine to help, but I never took it the way that I should have because the medicine made me even weaker. I wasn't the model patient to say the least.

Just when I thought I was about to come out on top, I was diagnosed with prostate cancer. I decided to fight that Goliath too, and I won, but I was left in a weakened state and my legs just didn't seem to work right after that. Now that was a real set-back for me. I never really recovered my strength after those treatments and found it quite hard to go about my normal daily routine. I kept pushing onward because I still had the green light in my spirit that said to drive on. The simplest of chores became very difficult, and I had to rest a lot. That really, really cramped my style.

Shortly afterward, I was told that I had bone cancer. I was about to celebrate my 78th birthday. My doctor said, given your circumstances, something else will take you out before this bone cancer does. I chose to take a shot each month to help strengthen my bones, but refused the pain killers after I found that they dulled my senses too much. I didn't want to spend the last times of my life living in a fog. I continued to hunt, fish, loaf around the area to all the flea markets and somewhat manage my chores. I just pushed through the pain.

I have now been living with bone cancer for three years. I've had stents inserted in my arteries so many times that I've lost count. Every time I got knocked down, I stood back up. I have fought hard for many years to remain standing. There was no peace in giving up the fight. That's why I kept fighting. I knew I still had work to do. The Lord knew that I wasn't afraid to die.

Friends and family have begun visiting me often. My family has spread word of my physical condition among the community and their extended families. I know that I am dying, and they do, too. I draw great pleasure visiting with them by the fire pit in the front yard, watching the multitude of grandbabies and great-grandbabies play in the yard, and being granted a time to grasp the hand of each of my loved ones so I can express my love for them. At the end of a visit, I choose my words of farewell carefully, doing my best to bestow blessings upon them. I now possess a peace that surpasses all understanding, and I have begun to live each day truly as if it is my last.

In the spring of 2016, my doctor found a tumor growing behind my right eye again. To remove the tumor, they would have needed to remove my eye. I had never recovered from the radiation treatments while I battled prostate cancer. Now, I faced more radiation treatments. I had some big decisions to make.

Margie used to say, "Jesus first, family next and then everything else just has to fall in line." I have spent over 60 years trying to understand her wise words. I don't know why I never took the time to ask her exactly what she meant by that statement before she died because she used it virtually every time I spoke with her. Margie had kindness, love for family and a peace about her like very few people I have ever met. The realization that one might have little time left on Earth forces a lot of introspection. Well, I have been staring death in the eye for a long time and I have had a lot of time to soul search. It hasn't been until the last 15 years that I have slowed down enough to ponder my life. Oh, don't forget to ask people what their motto in life really means. That way, you don't have to try to guess.

I wonder why I had ever been born to suffer such an injustice that Daddy beat me until blood ran down my legs or that I never had enough to eat. Why did such a wonderful, beautiful woman like my mother get stuck with someone like my Daddy? How could a man just up and leave three small children to fend for themselves? Why was I ridiculed and ostracized at school? If God is so good, why did He let all those bad things happen to me? It was hard to ignore truths that emerged from my heart while I stared death in the eye every day. I was forced to admit to myself that I thought God had dealt my family a bad hand.

I remember Fain being so angry at Daddy's funeral. They weren't tears of grief that streamed down his face, but tears of anger and bitterness. In my failed attempt to comfort Fain, I reminded him that we owed Daddy. "I don't owe him anything," Fain remarked. "He did nothing but bring us pain." I gently stated that if Daddy hadn't existed, neither of us would be here and none of our families would be either. At least Daddy did play a part in our being here.

I don't think Fain ever forgave Daddy for his cruelty, but he never really knew Daddy after he got saved and became a humble little man. Memories of the evils he had inflicted upon our family tormented Daddy for the rest of his life. I managed to forgive him, but those memories did still bring tears to my eyes. I realized that it's okay to cry over memories of wounds that produced scars. God wasn't offended by my reckoning and my blaming Him for the injustice we suffered. I think that just might be why Jesus bore His scars from the crucifixion. They served as a reminder of pain and triumph. A child never forgets acts of kindness, neither do they forget people who scar them. Always be kind to children.

As my soul-reckoning continued, I pondered the people that God had sent to rescue me. Why did Mrs. Wiggins feed us? Why did the Merita Bread man throw his stale products in the ditch? Why did Sam Craig feed us for a year while Daddy was in prison? Why did that old farmer take me in when Daddy had kicked me out of the house at eleven? Why did Margie and Pearl allow their wonderful, beautiful daughter Marie to marry a putz like me? She was just a child. Why did Marie stick with me all those years while I ran around being an idiot, leaving her at home to worry and raise six children? She labored from dawn until midnight every day making a home for my children while I galivanted about hunting, fishing, racing, flying, and pursuing my dreams. Had I also stolen her life as Daddy had stolen my Mama's? Maybe Marie, too, had the thought that God didn't play fair. Looking back, she has clearly been the greatest blessing in my life, and I have been her cross to bear. I could have done better. Marie sacrificed her whole life for me and her children. She was the cornerstone of the family and truly brought the stability that was needed. It was God who gave her the grace to endure. I know a great reward awaits her in Heaven as well as all the people God sent to rescue me. God does have a way of turning things around as Margie said, "God takes what is meant for curse and destruction and will turn them for a blessing!" That's exactly what God did for me and he used wonderful, obedient people. I realized that God had pieced my life together with blessing after blessing helping me recover from the blows sent to destroy me. God had been working all along from the first mustard seed prayer. That tiny seed planted at age four had grown into a mighty tree. I was forced to admit to myself that the bitterness toward my Daddy had blinded me from realizing that God had created a masterpiece using all the broken and missing puzzle pieces of my life. I felt like Abraham from the Bible. I realized that my offspring was almost as many as the sands on the sea shore and that God had blessed every aspect of my life, not to mention literally saving it many times. My family bore the same type of faith that I held, but even deeper. I thank Margie and Marie for teaching them faith.

"Jesus first," Margie insisted. She was convinced that Jesus sacrificed first so she could be blessed. "God has given me a Bible full of promises," she would say, "and He always keeps His Promises!" Margie could quote a scripture for every situation. When life appeared to be going to Hell in a handbasket, she assured us that everything would be all right. Her heart lived in a continual state of prayer. She really did walk and talk with Jesus. Jesus spoke, and she listened, and when she spoke, God listened to her. When things weren't going well in life, she reminded God of His promise about the situation and just ask Him to fix it. She left Him to the details. He would always turn the situation around somehow and work out the details for the best. Margie prayed about everything.

When Margie said, "Jesus first," she meant find out what Daddy God had already said and just trust Daddy to take care of it. She invited God into every situation of her life. No wonder she led her life in such a peaceful confidence. She knew that Daddy could and would fix anything broken in her life because her Daddy always kept His Word. I understand Margie's philosophy like this:

When my children were small, we traveled virtually everywhere in a motorhome. That was partly because someone always needed to pee or have a snack, and furthermore, there were eight of us in the vehicle including Marie and me. I decided very quickly that the easiest approach to traveling was simply to take the refrigerator and toilet with you. They played games, watched TV, or listened to the radio while sitting at the dining room table. When someone needed a nap, they just went to bed.

When I said, load up kids, they knew we were all headed for a fun adventure. The older kids packed a little bag of clothes and Marie and I took care of all the other details needed for a successful trip. When I reached the end of Cherry Road, I would ask them which way to turn. Sometimes we would end up in the Smokies and sometimes in Florida. Those long Colorado trips had to be carefully planned. The bottomline was, the children never had to worry about the food, the gas, or whether we had enough money to complete the journey. They never gave a thought about whether the vehicle would breakdown or that we might have a crash. They simply trusted Marie and me to take care of all the details. The kids knew we were off for a wonderful adventure, and all was well. They left all the details to us and boarded the land yacht without a care. That's the way I understand Margie's philosophy. She literally meant, Jesus take the wheel. Margie knew that her Daddy had all the details covered. I had to make decisions regarding the tumor that lurked behind my eye and God didn't seem to be speaking very loudly. I really needed Jesus to take the wheel and work out all the details.

It wasn't until my late thirties that I surrendered my life to Jesus and began to develop a deep, complete trust in Him like those people He had used to rescue me. They heard and obeyed the voice of God. I have finally learned to hear His voice and trust that God is always right despite a voice of reason that may sometimes discourage that obedience. Sometimes the things that God may ask us to do defies reason. Sometimes you must walk on water by faith trusting God to take care of all the details because His instructions may seem impossible to the mind. "He's a detail God!" Margie would exclaim. She had watched God take care of the details over and over even when He had to defy the laws of physics. He made those laws for us. She knew that nothing constrained her God.

It was God's hand that led me to play "Cat and Mouse" with my drunk Daddy so He could save Mama and my brothers. It was the courage He gave that allowed us to let the snake crawl across our tummies and pry apart those sunken barrels so we didn't drown in the Catawba. Why did that bullet not penetrate my skull when it penetrated that steel Army helmet? It was His softly spoken voice that led me to leave the safety of that foggy landing strip to rescue the distressed pilot circling Brasstown Bald when leaving the safety of the ground defied reason. It was God's clear instruction that sent me inching out the wing strut when the parachute lodged on the control stick steering my plane toward the mountainside. God had been trying His best to guide my steps and open doors to miracles all along when I simply obeyed His voice. It is for that very same reason that I have openly exposed my life to you in its failures and successes within the pages of this book. I have been given these fifteen years of reckoning so that perhaps you might learn from my struggles, triumphs, and mistakes. The knowledge of all mankind had been built upon the discoveries of the predecessors. Maybe your reading this book right now is not an accident. Perhaps I am your Mrs. Wiggins or your Merita bread man. God is real and furthermore, He can certainly be trusted. Learn to hear His voice. If you can't, ask Him to speak a little louder and listen again. He knows how to speak to His creation. Trust me, He will find a way to help you hear.

Remember, sometimes God speaks to the heart with a compelling urge like He did the day He sent me to rescue the struggling pilot circling Brasstown Bald with his tiny daughter on board his plane. What I did defied all my reason. We were all walking on water by flying blindly in the fog, but He made a way when there seemed to be no way. I trusted God with the details given one by one as we all walked out a miracle. The hard events of my life had prepared me to fly the path laid before me that day. Remember, my own son was in the plane with me. God not only showed Merlin who He was that day, but saved a father and his daughter. It is mind boggling when I think back. What if I had responded with a simple thought of reason. No, I am not going to do that. It's too dangerous. Learn to hear His voice. God always holds up His side of the bargain working out the details. He knows how to take the pieces of any puzzle and assemble them into a beautiful masterpiece. If a piece seems to be missing, He will fill in the gap. He is truly a detail God. However, He can only assemble the puzzle if you ask Him to. He is a gentleman who will never butt in or force His will upon yours.

That whole rescue was bigger than me. I did nothing but obey in yielding myself and my talents to His step-by-step instructions spoken to my heart. Like the willing Merita bread man, God took what I had to offer and placed it in the right place at the right time to produce a miracle, but I had to be willing to move in obedience. That story was truly like the miracle of the fishes and the loaves of bread in the Bible. Honestly, what are the chances that I would have bought a radio to put in my plane and be trying to install it just at the time those folks needed help? "Leave all the details to Him because He is a detail God!" Margie emphasized. Okay, I think I have that one figured out. God will move Heaven and Earth to keep His word. Maybe that lost pilot was a praying man, and God just used me and my talents to fill in his missing puzzle piece. It is important to respond to the nudgings of God.

"Family next," Margie said. I know I could have done better there. I spent a lot of time carousing with my friends, gallivanting about the country, and pursuing my dreams while leaving Marie to tend the children. My idea of tending the children was making sure they had motorcycles to ride, an old car to drive in the field or just bringing some sort of adventure to their life. I am just glad that none of them died on my watch. I taught them recklessness and lack of fear. They weren't afraid to try anything. In the process, they sniffed gas, drag-raced, played with explosives, wrecked motor cycles and cars, charmed snakes, and almost drown on numerous occasions. If it was dangerous, my children did it, but I let them be kids. Their lives were full of adventure, excitement, and fun. I am just glad that Margie and their Mama surrounded them with prayers for 24/7 angelic protection. My kids certainly taxed their guardian angels. Now I find myself praying as Margie for my grandchildren, great grandchildren, and great-great grandchildren since most of them inherited that reckless Ledford gene.

Rex praying a blessing over the family

"Family next," Margie said. If Margie meant to make sure the family never went hungry and always had a roof over their heads, well sure, I did that. I think "Family next" meant, be there for the family.

Marie grew up in a stable family and knew what stability meant. I didn't have a clue about stability. Nothing in my life had ever been stable. The only certainty in my life was that I was certain that Daddy would be drunk on the weekend.

Marie was the one who changed their diapers and beds, made them bathe and brush their teeth, helped them with homework, and tended them when they were sick. Marie was the one who magically prepared three fine meals each day feeding me, the kids and everyone else I had invited to the table that day. Marie was the one who asked me for lunch and paper money for the kids, and she was the one who scrimped and saved so the kids had Christmas. Marie was the one who truly made our house a home.

"Family next," Margie said. I have often heard Marie remind God of His promises over her children, grandchildren, great-grandchildren and now her great-great grandchildren calling them each by name. Marie and I have 34 direct line descendants. When you add in all the spouses, step-children and adopted children, calling them all by name, that is a lot of praying. I now understand why Margie prayed all the time. She had six very fruitful children too! I do believe that my kids monopolized Margie's prayer life because they were a lofty prayer assignment! My wife has turned into her mother, and that's a good thing.

Margie's famous words, "Jesus first, family next, and then everything else just has to fall in line." I used to think her phrase meant seek God's will, pray for all the kids, and then if you have any time left, pray about everything else on the list. I now understand that "And then everything else just has to fall in line" was her declaration of confidence that every detail of every situation she had discussed with Jesus had to line up with His promises to her. It was her way of saying that God would move Heaven and Earth to answer her prayer. She simply left all the details of change up to God. "He's a detail God!" she would proclaim with a big grin and the pointing of her finger. Now that's faith! Like I said, Marie has turned into her mother. I have often overheard Marie pray for me, especially in these last years when she watched me struggle so. It has pained her heart to watch my body deteriorate.

When approaching a red-light at an intersection, you had better stop or likely you may have a bad crash. If you have a green-light, you drive through the intersection without even slowing down. A yellow light means, it might be ok to proceed, but you had better slow down and look both ways before you do. Reaching a decision about battling the tumor growing behind my right eye was tough. I had already poured my heart into the pages of this book. My children were all successful, some retired and all watching their grand-children grow and thrive. Furthermore, they kept a close watch on Marie and visited often. They had taken over most of my chores and planned family workdays to take care of our home. I knew my children would take good care of their mother. There was no green light in my spirit as I faced my Goliath this time. I decided to take the path that would lead to peace. That was to simply let nature take its course. I refused to take anymore treatments in battling cancer. The doctors weren't pleased with my decision, and my family wasn't thrilled either. However, they knew that I had made up my mind. I had simply decided to let Jesus take the wheel. I knew He would work out the details.

"Growing old is not for the faint of heart." I've heard that saying all my life. It's true. The golden years aren't too golden as far as the physical being. I used to be as strong as an ox. Now, I just feel like an old broken-down mule that can't even plow anymore. I have been forced to stand and watch while all the younger and stronger mules plowed. I didn't like that humbling experience.

I wouldn't trade anything on this Earth for the last fifteen years as I have battled cancer and watched my family prove themselves. I would gladly battle affliction and pain to once again watch my six children take up the reigns. They have proven to me that Marie will be cared for even if I am not there to do so myself. I promised God while praying on Cherry Mountain in 1955 that if He gave her to be my wife that I would always take good care of her. I realized at that moment that it was God who had been taking care of both of us and our children all along and not me. In that revelation, I gained peace about leaving this Earth. I knew beyond any shadow of a doubt that God had taken care of all the details. All would be well, and it was okay for me to die.

That revelation reminded me of the times when I let my kids drive while sitting in my lap. I let them believe they were in control of the vehicle, but it was I who worked the gas and clutch pedals and sat ready to take the wheel at the first inkling of danger. I know Jesus has the wheel.

I've never tried this whole dying thing before, so I am thinking that the going may get kind of tough again, but it'll be ok. God knows that I never want to be a burden on my family. It's hard to practice dying, but I am thinking that I would like to just pass away like the old Indians did in those westerns I watched as a kid. You know, just go off in the woods and die. I hate that Marie and my family must sit by and watch as I try to stop living this old life. Either which way, it will be okay. I am boarding the motorhome with my Daddy trusting Him to work out the details of the journey. No worries for me.

I had it rough as a kid and it's a miracle that I even survived childhood. Since I met Marie, my life has been wonderfully blessed and filled with an unbelievable amount of joy and happiness. We've reared six beautiful, successful children. I have watched and helped rear grand-children and now even great-great grandchildren. I am satisfied with life and my decision. I am chasing after peace. God will give me the strength and courage to finish my course in this life.

My final words are first to my children. I know you will take care of your mother. Comfort her when I am gone and always keep a close watch on her. Make sure she has everything she needs and what she wants. Know that I am so proud of you and all your accomplishments in this life because you have made my heart proud. God has given me

some of the most wonderful children on the face of this Earth. You are a gift to mankind, and for that I am grateful. You are genuine, so don't be afraid to be real and share yourself in both failure and success. Always love on all the grandbabies and remind them of their Papa Rex by sharing happy stories with them. Above all, trust in the Lord and do good. He will order your steps. Love God with all your heart, soul and might and teach your babies to do the same. That way the blessings of God will continue to flow through the generations to come. Finally, never be too busy for family. That way, your mother's and my joy shall fill the Earth.

To you, Marie: You have shown kindness, love for me and your family like no other person I have ever known, even Margie. Please find it in your heart to forgive my shortcomings and insecurities. I guess I have been with you the way you are with Panda, that little dog: afraid to let her off the leash fearing she might run away. You have given your whole life for me and our children. I love you so much and I thank you for staying despite my trying to keep you on a leash. I now realize that I was trying to control my world. The one thing in life I could not bear was losing the one thing I loved most, and that was you. That was wrong of me, but it's too late to fix that. My prayer is that somehow God will make it up to you in the remaining years of your life. God always keeps His word, and my Daddy can and will fix what I have left broken. I will simply leave all those details to Him, because He is a detailed God.

God truly began to give my life meaning December 25, 1955. I will be peering through the windows of Heaven waiting for the most

beautiful woman I have ever seen once again. I am eternally grateful for your selfless love. Who would have ever thought it? My life truly began with just a wink and a little puckerdilly kiss! I will be waiting to wink at you from the choirs of Heaven. No, I will be waiting by the door with Margie to ask if I can show you home.

My Precious Marie, the most beautiful girl I have ever met!

20-Epilogue (From the Author)

My Father passed away April 19, 2017, one year after his doctor found the tumor growing behind his eye once again. Due to the hardening of his heart muscle, his oxygen levels continued to decline. He did however, insist upon continuing his daily routine as much as possible. His only complaint was that he felt useless. I never heard him mention anything about pain, but I cannot even imagine how badly his body must have hurt as he fought bone cancer. My family offered many prayers for him, especially about that tumor. We were all terrified that it would continue to grow causing excruciating pain. His doctor even called imploring Daddy to do something about the tumor so he wouldn't suffer greatly. Again, my father politely refused. He was simply following the green light in his spirit. He had peace about the whole ordeal. We didn't order an autopsy at Daddy's death, but we saw no physical changes in his eye over the course of the year.

My Father was the most stubborn man I had ever met. At first, he refused to wear his portable oxygen tank. He was embarrassed. Over the past few years, Daddy had established a routine of driving a 30-mile radius about his home, visiting thrift stores. As the year progressed, his oxygen levels continued to decline, and he began to lose consciousness. The episodes became more frequent. We were terrified that he would pass out and hit an oncoming car, and Mama worried herself sick anytime he left the house. The day he sneaked off and drove to the tractor sale in Blairsville, my brother Leroy resorted to informing Daddy that he was going to remove the motor from every vehicle on the hill if he didn't stop driving. Mama became his fulltime chauffeur because Daddy insisted that he make his rounds. Eventually, Daddy's oxygen levels declined to the point that he could hardly walk 30 feet without resting, even wearing his oxygen tank.

Mama strategically placed chairs about the home place so Daddy could slowly maneuver from point to point. She allowed him to maintain his routine while keeping a watchful eye on him. My mother rescued Daddy many times as he had fallen or passed out, coaxing him to breathe properly to regain consciousness. There were times that she couldn't get him back to his feet. My brothers or her grandson Casey, who lived just across the way, would rush to her aide putting Daddy on his feet again. My Father would have died much sooner had Mamma not rescued him repeatedly.

Daddy began to ride his four-wheeler all about the home place to maintain his routine. He hauled his oxygen in a little basket he had fastened to the front of the four-wheeler. Since Leroy and David were both retired, they were with Daddy virtually every day. He ordered them around the home place while they did his chores to his perfection. Because Daddy loved to sit by a camp fire, the pit in the front yard became his favorite hangout and everyone else's too. Family and visitors spent many hours laughing and sitting by the fire with Daddy as he recounted his unbelievable but true stories of his colorful past. My father enjoyed nothing more than spreading happiness and cheer, but we were all acutely aware that Daddy had limited time on this Earth.

Merlin had grown up to become the hunter in the family. Daddy loved to hunt, and always emphasize that "If you kill it, you have to eat it." When deer season rolled around last fall, Merlin erected blinds on his property on Myers Chapel and behind my granny Margie's house so Daddy could hunt. David or Mamma would take Daddy to Merlin's house, or Daddy would ride his four-wheeler to the blind behind Granny's. When Daddy killed a deer, Merlin dressed it, and then cooked it for him.

Turkey season opened April 8th in North Carolina. That was a brisk Saturday morning. Mama rose early with Daddy since he insisted that he go turkey hunting behind Margie's. He had been eyeing several big gobblers. The simple chore of putting on his hunting attire and preparing his rucksack exhausted Daddy, and he collapsed over the railing on the ramp we had built the summer before. Mama quickly retrieved a chair from the yard and caught Daddy in it as he fell backward. She struggled with his flailing arms, held his mouth closed, and forced him to breathe through his nose to inhale the oxygen from his tank. After five minutes, He regained consciousness. Mama had

Daddy in the blind wearing his oxygen

121

Daddy's last turkey
Grandson Aaron

saved him again. "You are not going turkey hunting this morning," She gently chided him. It was a rare occasion when Daddy agreed with Mama when she said that he couldn't do something. In fact, most of the time Daddy took such a statement as a dare.

"I think you are right," he calmly agreed, "But, I am going turkey hunting this evening!" Mama just shook her head and helped Daddy back inside. Sure enough, he went turkey hunting that evening. Although he didn't get a turkey Saturday afternoon, He did bag one the following Monday afternoon at Merlin's house. He gave the turkey to Ricky Cantrell who had grown up like Papa's grandson.

On Wednesday afternoon, nine days later, David tinkered with his $250 zero-turn mower while Daddy watched. He sat facing the big field across the road. Daddy always had a keen eye for game. In fact, he literally had one keen eye since he had totally lost vision in his right eye. Nevertheless, Daddy spied the biggest turkey he had ever seen as it strutted across the field in front of him. He yelled for David to take a closer look.

My brother recounted, "That turkey was so big that it looked like a hound dog walking across the pasture. Its beard was dragging the ground."

When David relayed his observation, Daddy exclaimed, "You fix the lawnmower without me, I am going turkey hunting!" Shuffling to his four-wheeler as quickly as possible, Daddy went to retrieve his gun.

Mama helped Daddy gather his equipment, and quickly sent him on his way to the blind because that trophy tom was headed straight toward Margie's. Daddy stopped at the garage and called David over to him. Daddy cupped David's huge hands in his and said with a big smile, "Give me some luck,"

David smiled back and said, "You know I have always been the unlucky one in the family Daddy. But, I give you all the luck that I have! Go take your prize!" That was about 3 pm on April 19th.

My teaching career consumed my life when school was in session, and there wasn't much time for playing. During the summer months however, we family made up for lost time. All of Daddy's children and grandchildren joined the fun. After our annual camping trip to the beach, I spent the summer with my kids playing, camping, and boating on Lake Chatuge. Mama and Daddy were always with us. Those were fun times. My campsite became the center of congregation. It reminded me of how we all gathered at Granny Cherrio's house on the weekend when I was a child. One of the grandchildren had coined Granny Margie's nickname and I was dubbed the K.O.A. queen. My tow behind camper always weighed 14,000 pounds because I took along anything and everything one could possibly need.

We had never owned a motorhome like Daddy, but Stan and I had always smiled and declared to each other that one day we would purchase one. After finally coming out of debt and paying off the mortgages on everything we owned, we could finally afford a motorhome. With my retirement in sights at June, I began the search for one. Visions of loading my grandbabies and simply heading off for an adventure filled my mind. It was the afternoon of April 19th when we agreed to purchase the big diesel pusher motorhome with all the bells and whistles. I was so excited to tell my Daddy about our new acquisition. We were headed back toward Murphy after our test drive, when the most magnificent rainbows I had ever seen filled the skies. There were rainbows everywhere. Even the clouds themselves were rainbows. I had never seen anything like it, and I have seen a lot of rainbows in my 55 years.

I had just settled to grade papers around 5 pm. I was thinking about calling Mama when she called me. "He's gone, Teressa" She managed through deep sobs. She furthered that he had gone turkey hunting. "I became so troubled in my spirit, that I went to Granny's to check on him. Teressa, I found your Daddy dead beside the turkey blind. He is still lying there. My cell phone wouldn't work, so I had to come back to the house to call," she continued. "I called the boys, and they are on their way. Merlin said he would call an ambulance." I began to cry the moment I heard Mama's voice because I knew Daddy had died. I pushed through the grief that sought to consume me, and did what I was compelled to do.

I began to pray with my Mama over the phone. "Lord, I know that my Daddy is with you right now, and that He is overtaken with the Glory his eyes behold. I know that Daddy is with You, Uncle Fain, and Granny. I know they are happy dancing and all is well. I thank You that Daddy struggles no more, and that He is stronger than an ox. But Lord, we need You to mend our broken hearts. We trust You to kiss our boo boos, and ease our pain. Bring the comfort and peace that only You can bring. Put Your arms around all of us, especially my Mama right now. Give us Your peace. I know that You hear us when we pray Father, and I thank You that we have exactly what we have asked. Lord, You have the wheel and You will see us through this. I am on my way, Mama." I quickly informed Stan that Daddy had died and that we had to go to Mama.

We arrived to find her alone, crying in the yard holding Panda on a leash. We both just wrapped our arms around Mama and we all embraced trying to squeeze away the pain. We cried together for an important moment, and then she said, "I can't get this silly dog to poop." We all laughed despite the tears that streamed down our cheeks. That was typical of my mom, and we both knew it. She always sought to break a tense situation with humor just like my father. I knew in that moment that Mama would be fine.

While I stood in the yard talking with her, the ambulance slowly drove up Cherry Road, past Mama's drive, and on to my granny's house 150 yards away. David was over there with Merlin, and Leroy arrived shortly thereafter. It was close to six by then. Mama continued to make phone calls to other members of the family including Daddy's close friends. A steady stream of loved ones began to arrive to comfort my mother. "I need to go see my brothers," I said to Mama.

"No Teressa. You are not going over there!" she commanded. I was taken aback by her stern voice. "I don't want you to see him that way. I don't want that to be your last memory of your daddy." At that moment, Mama could have asked me to do a back-flip off a cliff and I would have gladly obeyed.

It was dusk, and my niece Wendy was on her way from Atlanta. Wendy owns a funeral home and had promised Daddy that she would take care of all the details so Mama didn't have to do so. Wendy insisted that she stay the night with her, so I knew my mother would be in safe hands. I hugged Mama and headed home. Her home was full of loved ones. When I ventured outside to retrieve Stan, I found the yard full of people sitting around the fire pit talking, crying, and

124

laughing as they told stories of my daddy. That was a comfortable place for all of them.

It was almost dark when Stan and I finally headed toward our vehicle. "I need to go over to Granny's," I said to him.

"No," he replied. "You don't want that to be your last memory of your daddy." Stan had not heard my mom say the exact same words. He was protecting me, too. I relinquished. As Stan backed to turn around, I saw tail lights shining through the darkness above my granny's garden. At that moment, I succumbed to the grief. Stan just let it happen since he understood that pain, having already lost both of his parents. My three brothers retrieved Daddy's body from the woods and hauled it to the ambulance in Granny's front yard using Leroy's truck.

We had a short, sweet service the next morning at Ivie's Funeral home in Murphy, and then Wendy escorted Daddy's body to her funeral home in Atlanta for the cremation. All the brothers and sisters had originally planned to be there for the cremation, but when it came down to it, only Wendy, Maria and David had enough fortitude to carry through. The rest of us simply could not bear it.

My brother recounted what happened when they cremated my Father. They received a high-five from Heaven! This is his Facebook post about the event. "I want to share this with everyone. As most of you know, my sister, my niece, and I cremated my dad this evening. My sister Maria cut a small bundle of wild honeysuckle and placed it on Daddy's chest before we rolled him into the crematory. She reminded us that honeysuckle was his favorite flower because he loved the way it smelled. In the final stages of the cremation process, my niece Wendy opened the door to the crematory room and ran back up the hallway shouting for everyone to come to the crematory fast. Maria and I thought that something bad had happened, and we were alarmed. How wrong we were! When we ran into the room, the smell of wild honeysuckle overwhelmed us! It was as if we were standing in the middle of a patch of blooming wild honeysuckle. I could usually find a logical explanation for such a strange phenomenon, but there was none. However, there was no way to logically explain what could have caused this smell. That honeysuckle was consumed in the first five seconds of the firing of the furnace. I am 100% positive that this was my dad telling us that he was all right, and that there was no reason to be sad or grieve since he had passed away so sudden and unexpectedly.

I thank God that he allowed my dad to send us this message! I hope this helps others who knew my dad to get past the sadness and celebrate the life of a man so many loved and respected." After the events of that evening, we all began to plan my father's memorial to be held at the Georgia Mountain Fairgrounds three weeks later.

Wendy posted the obituary in the local paper, the Clay County Progress. I have never read an obituary that made me laugh aloud. It was perfect! "Mr. Rex Sanford Ledford 'Airplane Rex,' age 81 of Hayesville, North Carolina passed away peacefully, while turkey hunting on April 19, 2017. He was born on July 27, 1935 in Gaston County, North Carolina to Paul Franklin and Lucy Ann (Hooper) Ledford. From a young age, Rex had both an adventurous and determined nature about him, some may even say that he was fearless. No matter what challenge presented itself to him, if he wanted to do it, he did. Rex was a simple, yet brilliant man. He was the source of entertainment for many years in the local community, for he had perfected the arts of both daredevil flying and madcap racecar driving and was beyond exceptional at both. Rex loved the outdoors, for nothing made him happier than to be hunting in the mountains of Colorado, driving through the Great Smoky Mountains, or just simply fishing the Hiawassee River. Family adventures often included weenie roasts, bottle rocket wars, go-cart and motorcycle racing and last but not least, long rides with all the kids packed into the back of the car, accompanied by a gaseous stray dog, a loaf of white bread and hot potted meat. Rex was known and loved by many, many people and will be sorely missed. He is predeceased by his parents; Paul and Lucy Ledford and his brother Fain Ledford. Rex is survived by his brothers; Harold (Margaret) Ledford and Arlan (Janice) Ledford and sister-in-law Roberta Cherry Ledford. His devoted wife of 62 years, Marie Cherry Ledford. His six children; Maria Bryans, Judy (Ricky) Long, Leroy (Suzan) Ledford, Teressa (Stan) Woodard, Merlin (Marci) Ledford and David (Suzann) Ledford. His grandchildren; Rebecca (Todd) White, Wendy Eidson, Justin (Stacy) Long, Alecia (Ted) Derloshon, Josh (Megan) Woodard, Christopher (Tonya) Woodard, Jeremiah Woodard, Daniel (Hannah) Ledford, Casey (Krystal) Ledford, Michael Ledford, Jordan (Gabe) Jacobs and Aaron Ledford. His great grandchildren; Krista (John) Cunningham, Christian Sawyer, Emma Hyatt, Elizabeth Eidson, Madelaine Eidson, Bailey Derloshon, Tristan Derloshon, Tanner Derloshon, Benjamin Long, Silas

Woodard, Sawyer Woodard, Stewart Woodard, Samuel Woodard, Hannah Woodard, Brayden Woodard, Isabella Ledford, Adelaine Ledford, one great-great grandchild-Starla Riddle, and a multitude of other family and friends. A casual memorial service honoring the life and adventures of Rex Ledford, is scheduled to be held on Sunday May 7, 2017, from the hours of 4 O'clock in the afternoon, until 7 O'clock in the evening, so dress in your most favorite casual clothing and bring a chair for a time of reflection and storytelling. The memorial service will be held at The Georgia Mountain Fairgrounds (Campgrounds) 1311 Music Hall Road, Hiawassee, Georgia 30546. In lieu of flowers, the family has requested that you call the Hayesville School System Cafeteria (1-828-389-6855) and donate money to any child's lunch account that needs funding. Phoenix Funeral Services, Inc. has handled all arrangements." Wendy had no knowledge that this book contained information about the free lunch program when she wrote the obituary. It was another small confirmation that God was paying attention to the details. It is only one month after my father's passing that I write this epilogue. The lunch fund has already accumulated over $1,000. You may still contribute to the cause. No child should go hungry in this land of plenty.

We held Daddy's outside memorial/celebration of life service as planned at the Fair Grounds on May 7th, 2017. Although it had rained for a solid week, we awoke to cloudless deep blue skies. It was brisk, just like a Colorado morning. Upwards of 500 friends and family stopped by that afternoon to join the celebration. The entire family had joined forces to make the event happen. I think my family did a wonderful job at capturing and sharing the life of my father.

At one station, footage from Daddy's old 8 mm movies overlain with audio clips of Daddy telling stories played on a large display. What a precious treasure our father gave us when he took the time to film. Daddy's home movies proved that many of the stories contained within the pages of this book are absolutely true.

The slideshow, allowed folks to relive Daddy's life through a collection of pictures of him with family and friends. The photos went all the way back to Daddy's childhood. They were assembled into a slide show set to music remastered from Daddy's old vinyl record albums. I overheard many of the attendees laugh through tears commenting, I remember that day.

While the visitors enjoyed the media presentations, they snacked on snow cones, popcorn, nachos, hotdogs, and even bite-sized pieces of the last gobbler that Daddy had killed. What a nice tribute Ricky Cantrell paid in cooking that turkey to share. On the little hill behind the pavilion, many stood around the fire pit talking and laughing enjoying their snacks. Daddy's grandson Danniel brought a sweet message about the impact of my Daddy's first mustard seed prayer. We packed a lot of fun into that three-hour celebration. It was a bitter-sweet time.

Maria and David divided Daddy's ashes into small bags so that each of the children and grandchildren could spread them where they saw fit. So far, Daddy's ashes have been spread all about the home place, Tri-County Raceway, Andrews Airport, the catwalk at Chatuge Dam, Montana, Wyoming, and Colorado.

I know that my father is not gone, but simply away playing with Uncle Fain again. Until we all meet in Heaven, we branches of the mustard tree will continue to live life to the fullest as Papa taught us to do. Rex Ledford's legacy and stories live forever in our hearts and through the pages of this book. Our family will continue to gather around the firepit in the front yard to celebrate Papa's life. And, I have a motorhome! I wonder which way the grandbabies will have me turn?

Appendix – Margie & Extended Family

About the Author

Teressa Woodard is a twice Nationally Certified Secondary Mathematics teacher who earned her Bachelor's Degree from Western Carolina University and her Master's Degree from Piedmont College. After 29 years of teaching every math course from computer programming to Advanced Placement Calculus, she retired to travel and spend more time with her family. She and her husband of 36 years now have six grandchildren, two of whom bear the middle name Rex.

Made in the USA
Lexington, KY
19 March 2018